Birthmother:

The True Story of a 40-Year Search

Barbara Raye

Sam & Mary –
thanks you for taking
this journey with me.

Barbara R.

Birthmother:

The True Story of a 40-Year Search

Barbara Raye

For Deborah

Acknowledgement

This book could never have happened without the tireless efforts and patience of Dabinique Magwood. She walked me through every step of this entire process. She is my advisor . . . my editor . . . my publisher . . . and, hopefully, when this whole process if over, I will be able to call her my friend. Thank you, Dabinique. You have the perfect personality for the job that you do, and I appreciate every minute that you devoted to this book.

CHAPTER ONE

I can assure you, the last thing I was thinking about in the back seat of that '59 Chevy was "bringing disgrace to my family." No, I was not thinking about my family. I was not thinking about getting pregnant. I was not thinking about how fat I was or how unpopular I was or any of that negative stuff. All I could think about was how this really, really cool guy was making love to me. He must have really liked me if he wanted to have sex with me, right? I mean, how could you do that to someone if you did not like them? What the hell did I know? I was sixteen years old. When you are sixteen, sex equals love. At least it did back in 1959.

See, you have got to understand. I was fat. Not attractive at all. Certainly not part of the "in" crowd. No boy in my small hometown would ever date me. But low and behold, along comes this 19-year-old guy from upstate with this really hot car and sideburns and gorgeous brown eyes, and he asked me out. Me! He had no idea how unpopular I was. And I had no idea that his goal was to screw every teenage girl in the entire county. But even if I did know it, that would not have stopped me from going out with him. I mean, number one: He asked; number two: He was the coolest guy to ever hit town; and number three: Have you ever actually *seen* a brand new '59 Chevy?

The little town I lived in was about a two-hour drive from New York City. Today people take the train from that town and ride into the city to go to work every day. Today there is the internet and satellite television that connects every corner of the world with every other corner. But back in the 50's that two-hour drive from New York could just as well have been a two-*day* drive. We were so isolated we did not even *know* we were isolated. And, believe me, when you are sixteen years old and pregnant, the last place you want to live in is a small town. But there I was . . . two weeks after my one date with the '59 Chevy and I was starting to think I should be getting my period any day now. If you have ever been in that situation you know the routine. You are running to the bathroom every half hour to see if you started. Every twitch in your abdomen gives you that false hope that it is, yes, cramps, finally, only to be disappointed when it turns out to be nothing. Then, by the time you are five days late (and if you had a mother like mine) you *pretend* you got it. Then a few more days go by and you start telling yourself you just skipped a month. Nothing to worry about. You will get it next month, for sure. But the next month comes and goes and there you are, scared to death. Dying inside every waking minute. Sitting in class not even trying to concentrate. Riding the school bus staring out the window and wishing you were dead. Crying yourself to sleep every night. And, boy, the promises you make to God. You will promise anything if He will just let you get your period. But God must have been busy with something else.

What saved me from going completely mad during those days was writing to and getting letters from my girlfriend Jane. Jane lived in Yonkers, but we spent our summers at the same lake near Danbury, Connecticut and became instant friends from the minute we met in 1957. Jane and I were the same age so she was in no way equipped to give me advice. But she was there for me. In my letters to her I was able to pour out all the fears about the hell that had become my life. The depression was overwhelming. I had stopped praying that God would let me get my period. Now I was praying that the world would come to an end.

Telling my parents was not an option. Or at least I could not see it as an option. My father was extremely strict, and my mother was extremely prudish. Actually, *extremely* is not a strong enough word to describe either of them. Let me just say there was no way I could have told them. I just could not do it. And telling my sister was also out of the question, too. She was the perfect, goody-two-shoes and engaged to the perfect boy. The only thing on her mind was getting ready for her wedding. God forbid I take any attention away from her by getting knocked up. That would have been the most selfish act *ever*.

So, if I could not tell my parents or my sister, then I had to come up with another plan. Running away from home was the only solution. Because I was over-weight, I was not really showing in those early months. It was the only time in my life that I was glad I was fat. Even still, as the weeks passed, I found that by eating and eating and gaining even more weight, it made me feel as if I was buying time and hiding the pregnancy for as long as possible. My mother had already questioned whether I was really getting my period. She was used to seeing stained underpants in the laundry once a month from me and my sister. She suspected I might be lying or, as she put it, "Have you been doing something bad with boys?" Okay, she wants to see stained underpants . . . I will give her stained underpants. So once a month I would take a razor and cut the side of my heel until it bled and use the blood to stain my underpants. I do not know why I picked the heel. Maybe because I was looking for a place that would not show. Of course it hurt, but you do what you have to do. The hardest part was stopping the bleeding so it would not get on my bobby socks. I just remember scotch taping gobs of folded up Kleenex to my heel and having to walk around like that all day.

I figured I could make it until Easter vacation. I had gotten pregnant on November 25th in 1959 and Easter in 1960 was April 17th. Kind of late, but if I could just keep my secret until then I could spend Easter recess week at Jane's in Yonkers and from there, I could take off for Chicago rather than return home. Why Chicago? Well, I was looking for a big city to get lost in and at that time Chicago was the second largest city in the United States, second only to New York. All I knew of New York City back then was Times Square and Radio City Music Hall. I just pictured myself wandering around Times Square and running into my father, who would also be wandering around Times Square looking for me. Plus, no one would ever think to look for me in Chicago. I mean, who goes to Chicago? I told Jane everything about my plan only leaving out my selection of Chicago. I figured if she was really pressed for information she might crack and blow my hiding place. I let her think I was going to New York.

So, the planning began. I needed money. My father always carried lots of cash on him and when he went to bed, he would leave his wallet and keys on top of a hall bookcase. He just made it so easy. So at least once a week I would help myself to a five or a ten or a twenty. Whatever there was more of that I thought would not be missed. Then I had to figure out what to do once I got to Chicago. Back in the 1950's and 1960's there were magazines with titles like "True Confessions" and "True Romance". They all had stories about girls/women who were faced with incredible life-changing situations that were always a result of some sort of involvement with a member of the opposite sex. It was from one of these magazines that I read the story of a girl who had gotten pregnant and ended up being sheltered by the Salvation Army. So, then that became a very important part of my overall plan. Mind you, I had no idea if it were really true. Today you could check it out on their web site. Back in 1960 I had to trust a story in "True Romance" magazine. But it must have been true. They could not say it was true if it was not, right? At least that was how my sixteen-year-old mind worked. Kind of like the people who believe everything on the internet is true. Anyway, the plan so far was to go to Jane's in Yonkers for Easter recess . . . from Grand Central pick up a train to Chicago . . . once in Chicago contact the Salvation Army and let them take it from there.

I know when some people are in dire situations and they start to see solutions to their problems it can change their perspective and can almost be uplifting. However, this was not the case in my situation. I was still crying myself to sleep every night. I would wake up every morning hoping it was all a bad dream. The two or three weeks of morning sickness did not help. Waiting for the school bus was bad enough. But it was the hour-long ride that almost turned me green every morning. I was scared to death about what the future held. I was getting bigger every day. Even though I was overweight to begin with, it was getting harder and harder to hide my condition. I wore two girdles. I would wear pleated or full skirts and have to hike them higher and higher as my waist got bigger and bigger. But rather than wear my blouse out (a dead giveaway) I would tuck my blouse in and wear a large sweater over it to wrap around me, making sure I always complained about being cold. I would stay in my pajamas and bathrobe for as long as I could on Saturdays until my mother would yell at me to get dressed. When I got dressed for church on Sundays I would wait until the last minute so I could leave my bedroom with my coat on.

I spent almost all my time at home in my room. If I did come out to watch television in the evening I would get into my pajamas and robe first. At school, the hardest part was changing in the locker room for gym class. I would find a corner and try to keep my back to the other girls. Back in those days girl's gym did not exactly involve working up much of a sweat, so there were no communal showers to worry about. And I was not the only girl who left her half-slip on under her gym uniform, so that helped. But, quite frankly, the last thing I was worried about was having my classmates whispering about me behind my back. I had much bigger problems on my mind. If I could just survive until Easter vacation, I would never have to see any of these people again. So, to hell with them. To hell with everyone. God, I just wanted to die. I was so scared.

Easter finally came. It was a long day. The next day, Monday, April 18, 1960, I took the train to White Plains where Jane and her father picked me up. She was so shocked at my size and worried that her parents would notice. By then I was four and a half months along but being fat to begin with and still wearing a bulky cardigan all the time, made me feel like I was keeping my secret. The next day I went to a doctor in Yonkers just to verify that I was, in fact, pregnant. I had not had a period in five months. My middle was getting thicker and thicker. But it had never actually been *confirmed* by a medical professional that it really was true. So, Jane's cousin, Dorothy, made an appointment with her General Practitioner and the three of us went and sat in his waiting room for what seemed like forever. Dorothy was a nervous wreck, worried that someone she knew might see her and wonder what she was doing there. When they called my name, I was more worried about breaking down and crying than I was about the examination I was about to receive. And the reason I was not worried about the exam was because I had absolutely no idea what an internal examination involved. Not a clue.

The doctor was a kind, old Marcus Welby type. I almost relaxed when I saw him. He asked what I was there for and I told him I wanted to verify if I was pregnant. I can remember the first thing he did was look down at my ring finger. Not just glance at it. He actually *stared* at it. Up to that point it had never occurred to me to go to Woolworth's and pick up a fake wedding band. Note to self: Go to Woolworth's and pick up a fake wedding band. Dr. Welby showed me to the exam room and told me to get undressed from the waist down. I thought that was kind of strange since all he would have to do was check my belly. Then he told me to get up on the table. I sat on the side. Again, I thought it unusual that he wanted me to sit on the *end* of the table, but I complied. Sheet draped over my legs. Scrunch back. Put my feet WHERE????? What the hell is going on here? There was no nurse or assistant in the room with us. It was not required back then. Just me and Dr. Welby. I wanted to die I was so embarrassed. Little did I know it was only going to get worse before it was over.

When I left the examining room and paid the receptionist ten dollars for the visit, Jane and cousin Dorothy practically lunged at me. Jane asking, "What did he say? What did he say?"

And Dorothy begging, "Let us get out of here. Hurry. I don't want anyone to see me here." To answer Jane's question, yes, it was true. Dr. Welby confirmed that I was, in fact, pregnant. His exact words were, "Your womb is enlarged." Big mistake telling that to Jane and Dorothy. That became the buzz phrase for the rest of the day. "Would you and your enlarged womb hurry up? Do you and your enlarged womb feel like getting something to eat?"

Okay, so now it was official. I was pregnant. There was work to do. First, I needed a fake I.D. Here is how easy it was in 1960. Jane and I went to the Social Security office in downtown Yonkers. I filled out the form giving myself the name Barbara Roberts and adding two years to my date of birth, making myself eighteen years old. Eighteen seemed like such a magical age. You could do anything at eighteen and no one could stop you. I guess it was like twenty-one is now. I do not remember what address I used on the form, but it didn't matter. All we had to do was wait a few minutes for the card to be printed up and they just handed it to me. It is funny how you can remember how you actually felt and what was going on in your head so many years ago. But I can remember looking at the card when the clerk gave it to me and thinking, well, this is it. From now on I am Barbara Roberts. There is absolutely no going back. This is who I am now. This is who I am going to be for the rest of my life. I have actually changed my name. No do-over. I was in so much trouble. I was so scared. And I wanted to die.

The Saturday after Easter I said goodbye to Jane and got on the train headed towards Grand Central. I had a suitcase with me that must have weighed fifty pounds (pre-wheels, do not forget). When I got to Grand Central, I went to the information booth and asked how to get the next train to Chicago and was told that there was one leaving in less than five minutes. This was before Amtrak and before Metro North. I think now trains from New York to Chicago go out of Penn Station, but back then the line was called the New York Central Railroad and the trains went out of Grand Central. I can remember running for that train as if my life depended on it because, in fact, it did. When I got to the train, I jumped in the first open door I came to and sat down in the only seat left, a velvet chair. I was in the club car. The *club* car. When people use the cliché, "The smoke was so thick you could cut it with a knife" I realize it is just an exaggeration to make a point. However, in that smoke-filled club car that cliché would not have been far from the truth. The car was filled with grownups. All having a real good time. All carrying on as if they were already on their third or fourth or fifth drink . . . and the train had not even left the station yet!!!!

In the club car the chairs were not lined up in rows like the seats in a regular train car. These chairs all kind of faced the aisle with little tables in between them, so it was not as if I could sit and look out the window and ignore everyone else. My fellow travelers were mostly men in suits (on a Saturday), but there was this one girl, probably in her twenties, very attractive, traveling alone, and every man in the car was falling all over himself to buy her a drink. Not only was this girl pretty, but she had the most incredible hair. Straight, straight, straight, chin length, as shiny as patent leather, parted just slightly off center and covering half her face. And, boy, did this club-car girl know how to work that haircut. Every time one of the suits would say something even the least bit amusing, she would throw her head back and then forward again, so the hair fell all over her face. When she would shake her head, it was such an exaggerated shake that it took a full minute for her hair to stop dancing. And the more she did it the more the suits raved about what great hair she had. A few years later Vidal Sassoon became famous for *inventing* this haircut. I'll bet whoever gave club-car girl her hair cut was pissed when Vidal got all the credit. Meanwhile, I was sitting in my velvet chair, watching this girl, and thinking that she was the luckiest person on the face of the earth. She was pretty and thin, and men adored her, and she could flirt, and she was not pregnant. I ordered a coke. Nobody was offering to buy *me* a drink.

When the conductor came through the car to collect the

tickets, I paid cash for mine. I do not remember how much it was, but it was a lot. I left home for Yonkers the day after Easter with $240 in my wallet. That amount was starting to shrink faster than I had anticipated. In 1960, to a sixteen-year- old, $240 was a lot of money. In the real world it was not. But I knew I had enough to get to Chicago and then I would be saved by the Salvation Army, so I was okay for now. It was several hours later that the conductor suggested I move to another car. I do not know what took him so long, but I was glad to get out of that opium den. So, me and my fifty-pound suitcase made it from car to car until I found a seat all to myself. It was going to be a long night. Other than the girl with the haircut I do not remember much about the ride. I must have gone to the dining car for supper and breakfast, spending more of my dwindling bankroll. The only stop on the way that I can remember seeing was Kalamazoo, Michigan. One of the last records I bought before I left home was a Steve Lawrence/Edie Gormet album that had the song *I've Got a Gal in Kalamazoo* on it and, what do you know, it is a real place. And I will never hear that song again because I did not bring the album with me.

CHAPTER TWO

I can remember pulling into Chicago. I did not want to get off the train. Why couldn't I just stay on the train and ride it forever? But that was not an option. When I walked out of the train station the first thing that caught my eye was a big sign on the front of a very old hotel that advertised rooms for something like four dollars a night. So, I walked from the train station right next door to the hotel lobby. When I said I wanted a room the person behind the desk asked if I wanted a private bath and, of course, I did. Well, that would be $7.50 a night. I took it.

The room was very small and very old. I think the window faced an air shaft. I sat on the bed and cried and cried and cried. I did not think I was going to be able to stop. I was hungry and wanted to go outside to find some place to eat, but I could not stop crying. I think I slept in my clothes that night. I did not have to ask myself how I had gotten into this horrible situation. I knew exactly what I had done to get there. There was no one to blame but myself.

The next morning, I was able to pull myself together and hit the streets to look for a diner or (this will take you back) an automat. I do not remember where I ate, I just remember thinking there was really no rush to call the Salvation Army. I mean, I knew I was going to have to get in touch with them soon, but not this day. I had a place to sleep. I had some money left. I just needed a day to collect my thoughts and get my story straight. I walked up and down State Street and went to see a movie. When I got out of that movie, I went to another one. I got something else to eat and went back to my room, got in bed and cried until I fell asleep. The next day I pretty much repeated the same thing. Eat . . . two or three movies . . . and cry myself to sleep. In fact, I did the same thing every day for an entire week. And then I ran out of money. It is funny how something from so long ago can still be such a vivid memory. I can remember having seven cents left to my name. I bought a nickel Hershey bar and two of those little penny Hershey bars that they do not even sell any more. I ate the nickel bar one day and the next two days I had one of those penny candies each day. And then I called the Salvation Army.

As it turns out, you cannot just walk up to the front door of the Salvation Army Emergency Shelter for Women and Children. You need to be *referred* . . . or at least you did back in 1960. Over the phone I told them my story. That I was eighteen; my mother was dead; my father beat me; so, I ran away. The woman on the other end of the phone referred me to the Traveler's Aid Society, which had an office over in the train station. So, I walked over there, found the office, and waited my turn. I was an absolute nervous wreck. And it did not help that some guy in the waiting room decides to tell me his tale of woe. How he and his wife and their three kids were on their way down south or up north to look for a job and his wife just took off and took what little money he had and left him with the three kids, one of whom was a baby not more than six months old. (I wonder if the wife's name was Lucille?) He seemed like a nice enough guy, but, quite frankly, I had problems of my own. And it did not help that, as he's telling me his story, the six-month-old spit up on me. I had never seen anything so disgusting.

When my time came to meet with the Traveler's Aide woman, I had my story down pat. I had repeated it so many times to myself that I was prepared for any questions she could throw at me. One shocker, though, was when she told me I would most likely have to go back to New York State. Not to live with my father, she explained (because I was eighteen, she thought), but simply because I was not yet twenty-one. But in the meantime, she would refer me to the Salvation Army's emergency shelter since the hotel I was staying at (at $7.50 a night) was just too expensive. So, she told me to pack my suitcase, pay my bill, and come back to their office in the train station and she would get me to the shelter. I then went back to my room, packed my suitcase, and walked out the side door of the hotel. I still owe them the money for the week I spent there.

I kind of had a mental image of what the shelter would look like from reading the True Confession magazines. I pictured something like a white colonial house. Tastefully decorated. Filled with teenage girls like myself who were all really nice young women who just made a stupid mistake. Sweet, compassionate grandmotherly-type staff. Lots of hugs and "There, there. Everything is going to be alright." So, when the car service pulled up to this awful looking building my first impression was that, just maybe, I had made a mistake in thinking the Salvation Army was, in fact, going to be *my* salvation. Then when I walked inside and saw this horrible, gray-walled institution and heard the sounds of heavy doors being slammed and the echo of yelling being bounced off a stairwell wall, and when I saw the peeling paint and metal furniture, I just *knew* I had made a mistake.

When I walked in the door of the Salvation Army Emergency Shelter for Women and Children the staff was waiting for me. Like I said, I was expecting somewhat of a warm welcome. Kind of a "what can we do to ease you though this troubled time in your life" sort of attitude. But I did not get it. Now that I think back, I just represented more work for them to do. I mean, the name of the place really explains their attitude. It is an *emergency* shelter. Not a haven where long stays are the usual. I am guessing the women and their children were in and out of there faster than the sheets could get laundered. What would be the point of wasting a smile on any of them? They knew I was pregnant, but since I had told Traveler's Aide that I was eighteen, I was not really classified as a runaway. They had me take my suitcase to a room on the second floor that I would share with a 55-year-old woman. She was sitting on her bed when I walked in the room. I can remember she had a slight odor, but not so bad as to pose a problem. I do not remember what her story was. I know she told me how she ended up there, but I could not focus on anything she was saying. It was all I could do to take in this dark, drab, austere room with its metal furniture and bare walls. It looked more like a prison cell than a *shelter*.

I was not there long when an announcement was made that dinner was being served. The 55-year-old showed me where we had to go. I will never forget walking into that dining room. The tables were set, and dessert was already at each place. It was two canned pear halves in a blue Melmac bowl. Even though I had not had anything to eat since the one piece of Hershey penny candy the day before, I can remember being so repulsed at the whole institutional look of the dishes and the furniture and the food.

In the dining room I got to see all the other residents. Young mothers with two and three children, and a few young and middle-aged women without any children in tow. I do not know how many residents there were. Twenty, maybe thirty. I was so overwhelmed with my own situation that I really did not care what anybody else's problem was. I just knew I was at the lowest point of my young life. As of this writing I am 75 years old and I can now look back and honestly say, for sure, that the days I spent at that shelter were, in fact, the lowest and most dismal circumstances I have ever had to live through. If I had been older or more mature, I could have seen that place as just a temporary location and I would have realized that this was not going to be forever. But when you are sixteen, pregnant and a runaway, it is hard to see even five minutes ahead. I just knew I could not live like this. I knew no matter what hell I was going to face, I had to go back home.

The next day I was sent back to the train station to meet with someone at Traveler's Aide to work on my situation. Because

I was referred by Traveler's Aide, I became their client or case or, more realistically, their problem. And because I was *eighteen* and still had more than four months to go before my due date, I would have to get a job. A job!!! They wanted me to go to work!!!??? This was 1960. Back then most pregnant women quit work in their third month. Even office workers. What on earth *job* were they going to find for me? The only job I had ever held was working in my father's store. It is a whole different world out there when your boss is not your father. I was terrified. However, even though I had made up my mind to make a full confession to the Traveler's Aide case worker, about one percent of me was kind of curious as to what kind of work they might come up with for me. Maybe having a job would make it possible for me to be self-sufficient, keep my baby and, more importantly, keep from having to face my parents. So, I briefly played out Plan B, where I stayed in Chicago, got a job, had my baby, got a small apartment, in a run-down part of town, with rats and bugs, living on welfare. So much for plan B.

I do not know how long I had to sit in the Traveler's Aide waiting room. However long it was, it was not long enough. I can remember thinking if I sat there long enough the world might come to an end. But eventually I was called into the case worker's office and she started talking before I even sat down. She was talking about me going back to New York and working with the Traveler's Aide there to get me situated, but as soon as she stopped to take a breath I said, "I lied to you." Funny, she did not look surprised. So as best as I could talk through non-stop crying, I told her my name was not Barbara Roberts. I was not eighteen years old. My mother was not dead. I ran away from home. The only thing I had told her in our first meeting that was the truth was that, yes, I was pregnant.

I thought I was living in hell before. The pre-confession part of this journey was like paradise compared to what lay ahead. At least I did not have to tell my parents. God bless Traveler's Aide, that was *their* job. I was sent back to the shelter to await my sentencing. I had not stopped crying since I blurted out "I lied to you." I just could not stop. Later that day one of the Salvation Army social workers called me into an office and updated me on what was going on. My parents had been told. My father was sending, via Western Union, the money to cover my train ticket back. Through Catholic Charities they had secured a bed for me at a home for unwed mothers down in New York City. However, this was the end of April and the opening at the home would not be available until the middle of May.

I had no idea how I was going to survive at home for two or three weeks. I mean, that is where my parents live. I wanted to die. I did not want to get on that train home. Why couldn't the entire world just explode? If I thought it was a mistake to tell the truth, I knew it was too late to turn back. And all the time, on top of this horrible depression, was that overwhelming feeling that I had gotten myself into this situation. No matter what hell I was going through, it was nobody's fault but my own.

I spent another night at the shelter and the next morning I was sent back to the train station for my final meeting with Traveler's Aide. The case worker, in full navy-blue uniform with badges and identifying patches, walked me to the train, holding my arm the entire way. I do not know if she thought I was going to bolt or if this was standard procedure or what. I can just remember thinking how unnecessary it was.

So, we got to the train and just as I am about to board, I heard someone call out, "Barbara?" What the hell? I do not know anybody in Chicago. That was the whole idea of going there. I turned around to see Richard, a young man from my hometown. We lived a tenth of a mile from each other. His sister was a friend of mine. I thought I was going to die. He was in a sailor's uniform. He was heading back home on the same train I was about to take. He could not miss the case worker with all the badges and patches. His first question was, "What are you doing in Chicago?" And without skipping a beat, I said, "I was here visiting my aunt."

Once on the train it did not take Richard long to realize

visiting my aunt most likely was not the truth . . . unless my *aunt* worked for Traveler's Aid and walked me to the train gripping my arm. When I sat down Richard sat next to me, making me feel rather uncomfortable. It was bad enough that I was trying to hide this secret under my raincoat. But more awkward than that, he was my friend's really cute older brother and I always had a tiny crush on him. Not a serious crush. Just one of those crushes where if I was at my friend's house and he was home I would act stupid and feel self-conscious. So, the first thing he said to me with a smirk on his face was, "You were not visiting an aunt, were you? I'll bet you ran away." He was right. I ran away. I explained that things were hell in my house, what with my sister getting married and she was getting all the attention and I was just in the way and could not do anything right, while she was just this perfect person.

Surprisingly, Richard sort of understood. He was the second oldest of four children and for some reason he was always the one in the family that was getting in trouble. Nothing serious. Just not living up to his parents' expectations. His two sisters were just perfect, and I can remember we talked about how hard it is to live up to those standards. I do not know what he was doing in Chicago. Maybe there was a Navy base near there. I just know I had to keep my raincoat on for the entire trip.

I believe they did have sleeper cars on the train, but they cost more than the standard ticket, so I got to spend the overnight ride sitting up. It was a long trip, but not long enough. The closer we got to the border of New York State the more nervous I became. I was worried about seeing my parents at the Poughkeepsie train station. I was worried about my parents seeing Richard get off the train with me and wondering if he knew my secret and now the whole town would know. Quite frankly, my main concern was how in God's name I was going to deal with my parents. I honestly couldn't care less about who in our small town knew. What did I care? It's not like I planned to spend the rest of my life there. All I had to do was get over this one little problem and then I could lay out a plan for the rest of my life. On the other hand, I was hoping I would just die on that train. If I died on the train I would not need to deal with my parents at the other end. Keep in mind, though, there is a big difference between wanting to die and trying to commit suicide. As I see it, they are two totally different emotions or desires. Besides, it takes time to work out all the plans of a suicide. I did not have a lot of time.

The train pulled into Poughkeepsie. Before I even left the train, I saw both my parents standing on the platform. I will never forget the look on my mother's face when she saw Richard walk off the train with me. She could not even talk. My father managed to say hello to him and ask if he needed a ride. Richard insisted his parents were on their way. My mother kept staring at my raincoat to see if or how much I was showing. *Oh my God. Does Richard know? Now everyone in town will know. Oh my God. How will she be able to show her face out in public again?* I just knew what was going on in her head. But, still, she said nothing. And there was no *welcome back* embrace or a kiss on the cheek. Not unusual, though. I never had a warm, fuzzy relationship with either of my parents. There was not a lot of hugging in our household. Actually, it would have been better if they *had* hugged me when I got off the train, because then I would have been so shocked at this sign of affection that the shock would have killed me, and all my problems would have been over. Instead, we walked to the car in silence.

I am guessing my parents worked out the scenario before they picked me up because my father told me to sit in the front seat of the car and my mother sat in the back. We left Poughkeepsie in silence. Once we got out of the city my father finally started talking. He said in a very matter-of-fact tone of voice, "So now you're in trouble." I snapped back, "I'm not *in* trouble. I'm pregnant. Pregnant! Can't you even *say* the word?" Keep in mind . . . I said that in my mind, not out loud. My father went on to explain what was going to happen. He said I would be going down to New York City to a shelter for unwed mothers that is run by Catholic Charities. (Oh my God. There is a God. I am going down to New York City!!!! This is perfect. Not only will I get out of my parent's house, but I get to spend the next four months in New York City!!!!! Hallelujah!) Of course, this was not going to happen for a couple of weeks yet. (Shit!) They had to wait until there was an opening, but it should be around the middle of May. Christ. That was over three weeks away. I could not spend three weeks in the house with my parents. My father said I would be going to school at the shelter so that I could finish my junior year there.

Meanwhile, I was not to leave the house. I was not to talk to any of my friends on the phone. I was not to have any friends over to the house. If any of them wanted to know why I could not see them I was to tell them I was grounded and being punished for running away. That was the first time I found out that the entire town knew I had run away. I just figured it was something between me and my family. I had no idea *the town* was involved. When I asked my father if people knew that I had run away he explained that there was a thirteen-state bulletin that went out on me. They took pictures of me out of my scrapbook and gave them to the state police. They even questioned some of the kids I went to school with to see if I had mentioned what I was up to and where I might go. Gee. For the first time in my life, I got a whole bunch of attention and I was not even there to enjoy it. Bummer.

My mother was absolutely crazy once we got to the house. It was broad daylight, and you could tell she was so worried that someone might see me and my raincoat and wonder, *could she be?* I just remember hating walking into that house. I put my suitcase in my bedroom and just sat on my bed and cried. With my father out of ear shot my mother finally opened her mouth. And, boy, did she ever open her mouth.

"You *should* cry, young lady. Do you have any idea what a *disgrace* you are to this family? How *could* you do this? You are lucky Erick still wants to marry your sister. A lot of boys would not even want to get *involved* with a girl if they knew she had a sister who did what you did. You are damned lucky he hasn't backed out of the wedding. How do you expect me to show my face in this town again? Did you tell Richard on the train? You had better not have. I just hope to *God* he did not notice what you look like under that coat. How in the *hell* did you get so big so fast? And everyone is going to expect to see you in church on Sunday. How are we supposed to pull *that* off? I will tell you how. You are going to put on every girdle you have and wear your gray suit. And do not even think for one minute that you are going to keep this thing and bring this thing into this house. You know what they call things like this? They call them *bastards.* That is what this thing will be. A *bastard.* I swear to *God* I will never forgive you for this. I don't know how we're going to get through this." And on and on and on. Not just that first day home, but any time it was just the two of us in the house. If she was trying to make me feel like the worst person who ever walked the face of the earth, she did a pretty good job of it. What she did not know was anything she said to me or any name she could call me I had already said to myself, only ten times worse.

I was so scared about what was ahead for me. I was afraid that I might actually have to give birth. I had no idea what the shelter in New York would be like. Were the people who ran it going to be mean? Were the girls there going to be lectured constantly about how horrible they were? Was it going to be like Chicago? I was a nervous wreck about going to the shelter, but on the other hand I could not wait to get out of my parent's house. I just wanted to run away. Oh . . . I forgot . . . I already tried that.

CHAPTER THREE

The call came around the middle of May, just as expected. The shelter had an opening. We were on the road in no time. I think I cried all the way to New York City. I will bet my parents thought I was crying because I did not want to leave home. If that were the case than I would have been crying tears of joy. No, I was crying just because I did not know what was ahead. The Salvation Army shelter out in Chicago was so depressing. I assumed all shelters were like that. But when we got to the city at the *secret* entrance on the side of the New York Foundling Hospital, the girl who greeted us was pleasant. A housemother met us and took me and my mother upstairs while my father waited on the ground floor. Men were not allowed on the shelter floor. Getting off the elevator and walking down that long hall to what would become my room for the next three months was almost a pleasant surprise. No chipped paint. No gray walls.

The bedrooms all had a sink just as you walked in the room. Since the doors opened in, if someone were standing at the sink they would be in the way of the door. So, my first introduction to my new roommate, who was standing at the sink, was to have the housemother hit her in the side with the door. I still remember how pretty she was. Beautiful long, black, shiny hair. Exquisite eye makeup that almost made her look Asian. And, except for being eight and a half months pregnant, she was slender and fit.

We were introduced by the housemother. I think she was a couple of years older than I was. My mother could not wait to get out of the place. I do not think we even hugged goodbye, but that was not unusual under any circumstance. After my mother left, I sat down on the bed and cried. Not because I was sad to see my mother go, but because I was nervous about what the next three months were going to be like. One of the other girls came by the room to see my roommate. When she saw me, I can remember her asking my roommate why I was crying. Her answer was, "She just got here." The other girl understood perfectly. I guess they all cried when they first got there.

At some point I met with the housemother so she could tell me what life at the shelter would be like. All the girls were responsible for making their own beds and keeping their part of the room clean. We had to do our own laundry. We could not come to breakfast in our pajamas. Chores were assigned, but they were light. I think it was something like taking turns setting the dining room tables. Nothing overwhelming. After all, we were all "with child." And, of course, since I was still in high school, I would have to take classes every day. They had two teachers who came to the shelter. One taught math and science and the other English and history. I think there were only one or two other girls finishing up the school year. I was surprised that I was one of the youngest girls there.

I can remember being nervous about meeting the two schoolteachers. I mean, they were *teachers*. Teachers are judgmental and hypocritical, without a compassionate bone in their body. It never occurred to me that these two women might *not* be judgmental and might *not* be hypocritical. And it never occurred to me that, just maybe, I was not the first pregnant student they had come across. Of course, once I met them all my fears were eliminated. One was just a sweet, matronly woman, probably in her fifties. Wearing the mandatory floral-printed dress required of every fifty-year-old schoolteacher back then. She looked like every other middle-aged teacher I had grown up with.

The only difference was that she was actually pleasant. The other woman was, well, I do not know, maybe she was more the typical New York City teacher. She was also in her fifties (I am guessing), with hair dyed blue-black; blood-red lipstick; and enough compact powder on her face to rival a rodeo clown. And . . . as I walked in the little room the first time I met her, she was applying *more* of this powder. Was she in the witness protection program and trying to completely disguise herself by painting another face on top of her own? And she had the thickest New York accent I had ever heard. More like Bronx or Brooklyn. One of the things high school girls like to do is make fun of their teachers. Damn. I did not get to do that. It would have been so much fun.

I was surprised to find out that hardly anybody made it to the shelter when they still had over three months to go like I did. Most of them had less than two months before their due date. But everyone's story was different. There were probably, I am not sure, fifty girls/women at the shelter at any given time and that meant there were fifty different stories. I was the only former runaway. There were a few other teenagers there, but they were constantly getting visits from their parents. There were two nurses. Not employees . . . residents. There was an 18-year-old who lived only a few blocks away who *never* went outside. There was a 13-year-old who had gained over a hundred pounds who seemed to have the mental capacity of a seven-year-old. There was a girl who was going through her *second* out-of-wedlock pregnancy. There were a lot of women in their twenties from all over the country who ended up in New York City to hide. I guess, if you are not from New York and you have no family or friends there and you are pregnant, even though you've been able to find a place to live during the early months of your pregnancy, I guess you had to find some place to stay towards the end before you deliver. And that was where the secret entrance of the New York Foundling Hospital came in. I became fast friends with one of the girls who sat at my table in the dining room. She was in her early twenties and from Florida. I do not remember what her real name was because I called her Connie. I called her Connie because she looked like a Connie. And she did not mind at all. Everyone at that place had so many secrets that being called by the wrong name was really no big deal. I would take my classes in the morning (usually it was just me and the teacher) and after lunch Connie and I would spend our afternoons together. Sometimes we would go out for a walk. Once we even made it all the way over to Central Park. Sometimes we just sat around the shelter living room. Neither of us ever had any visitors so our days were always free.

There was a small group of girls who were into the afternoon soap operas so that's when Connie and I would just hang around the little kitchen that was there for the girls' personal use. And then there were the doctor's visits and chores and laundry and breakfast, lunch and supper. The days went by fast. I do not remember ever being bored. Every few days someone would go into labor and leave to have their baby, never to be seen or heard from again. I was there so long I went through five or six roommates. Every one of my roommate's story was different. They were all older than I was. The other girls in the shelter would ask me if I felt bad because my roommates would come and go, and I was still there. Truth was, I never wanted to leave. As long as I could stay there, I didn't have to return home and deal with my parents. I did not have to worry about what the kids in school would say when I went back. I did not have to worry about what anybody in my small town was saying about me. But mostly it was the dread of going back home. Especially since my sister was getting married at the end of the summer which would leave me alone in the house to deal with my parents. Oh, and speaking of my sister's marriage . . . her wedding was scheduled for August 27th. My due date was August 20th. Not too much pressure.

Less than two weeks after I arrived at the shelter, I turned seventeen. I didn't say a word to anyone. I don't know why I wanted to keep it a secret. I just knew this was not the time or the place to "celebrate." I can remember all day just wishing this day would end. Birthdays are supposed to be joyous occasions. You are supposed to spend your birthday celebrating with family and friends and getting presents and being treated special. You are not supposed to spend it pregnant in a shelter for unwed women. I had a radio in my room. I can remember being alone in my room getting ready for bed and hearing Tony Bennett sing *Put on a Happy Face* for the very first time. At the end of that song he says, "Smile. It's your birthday." That was all it took. I burst into tears. Just feeling sorry for myself.

I was able to pull myself together when someone knocked on my door. It was one of the other residents telling me Sister Mary wanted to see me, "Why? What did I do?" (I figured I was in trouble about *something*.) The other girl did not know. Just that Sister wanted to see me down in the community room. As I walked down the hall I could see into the back of the room and could see other girls sitting at the tables. That was a relief. It was not just me in trouble. It must have been some kind of gathering of all the girls for some announcement. That had been done a couple of times in the past two weeks to make sure all the residents knew about maybe a change of schedule or some issue that needed to be addressed. So, it was nothing to worry about. When I walked in the room everyone yelled, "Surprise!" At *me*. ME!! It was a surprise birthday party for *me*. I had only been there a couple of weeks and, since nobody else had a birthday during that time, I did not realize they did this for every girl's birthday. It was wonderful. Absolutely wonderful. I never felt so special before or since. There was a cake and snacks. We played bingo and I even won one of the games. My prize was a little, soft doll, about the size of a Beanie Baby. I wish I still had it.

It was a long time ago, so I do not remember every detail of every day that I spent at the shelter, but I do remember the day I found out how I did on the New York State Algebra Regents. It must have been late June because my classes were over. I had taken the regents exam a few days before and really could care less as to what grade I got. But this one afternoon I was sitting in the living room. It was between lunch and dinner so there were quite a few girls in there. Knitting, reading, watching television, smoking or just talking. And since the living room was the only place at the shelter where smoking was allowed, some girls would go in there just to have a cigarette. Yes, smoking. This was 1960.

The powder-faced teacher came into the room and stood over me and said, "Did you hear how you did on the math regents?" I told her I had not. She said (nice and loud), "You *failed!!!!* I thought you told me you were good in math. I gave you a passing grade for the year and you *failed* the regents." Everyone in the room stopped what they were doing and looked at her and then looked at me. I did not have enough to worry about, and now this embarrassment!!!!??? Thanks a lot, Mrs. Powder-face. She could not have called me into the classroom to tell me this. No . . . she had to make an announcement in front of everyone. *FUCK*!!! I probably turned four shades of red. I know I was humiliated. I felt like the stupidest person on the face of the earth. As I look back now, I realize with all the drama and trauma going on in my life at the time it was not the worst thing that could happen to me. I mean, after all, I did *pass* the class, just not the regents. So, I would not get a regents' diploma when I graduate. Not exactly at the top of my priority list at the time. But still . . . I was embarrassed in front of all the other girls.

Now that I think back, I do not remember how the other high school girls did. It is not like we hung around together the way girls do in a real high school. Since I spent most of my spare time with Connie, I did not get too close to any of the other girls. I mean, we did not exactly plan to keep in touch and stay close friends forever. It was not that kind of atmosphere. In fact, there's only a handful of girls that I can still remember, and most of them were the ones who lived in New York City and were afraid to leave the shelter for fear of running into someone they knew. There was this one girl, in her 20's, who told her family that she was working down in Florida. But she made the mistake of telling them that she went to the beach every weekend because she thought that was what people in Florida did. So, every morning that the sun was shining she would go out onto this brick, east-facing fire escape and take her top off and face the sun in her bra trying to get as much of a tan as she could, hoping that the bra straps would look like bathing suit straps.

Another girl, one of the RN's in her 30's, would take a chance and wander outside once in a while, but she always wore a raincoat, head scarf, sunglasses and would hold a handkerchief over her nose and mouth as if she were getting ready to cover a sneeze. But with that getup, in the middle of summer, and being almost six feet tall, I am wondering if she did not bring *more* attention to herself. I, myself, always wore a coat when going outside, no matter how hot it was. I think all the girls did. We were so embarrassed about our condition. Today unmarried celebrities proudly show their baby bumps, and everyone is excited for them. Even non-celebrities almost brag about being a single mom as if it is a badge of honor. When did we cross over from being disgraced unwed mothers to being proud single moms? It was a different time back then.

The one place outside the shelter we could all go and feel totally safe from the world was the chapel. It was on the first floor, an addition to the main chapel, and was built off to the side, with the pews facing the side of the alter. The main, supposedly larger, chapel faced the alter, but people in that section could not see who was in that little side section, and, of course, we could not see them. Even when we went to communion, we could not see each other. Back then communion recipients would kneel along the railing facing the alter, not receive standing up like they do now. I am guessing the whole chapel was designed when the hospital was built. As we were told, this was not the first New York Foundling Hospital. The original was a block or two away and proved to be too small at some point. So, I imagine when the new building was designed it was decided to address the chapel issue so that the unwed mothers could attend mass without being seen by the rest of the congregation. All I know is it was a very peaceful refuge. I went to mass every morning before breakfast, as did about a dozen other girls. I think I was hoping to earn some forgiveness for this horrible, horrible thing that I had done. Not forgiveness from my parents, mind you. But forgiveness from God. That was the way my mind worked back then.

I said I never had any visitors for the three and a half months that I was at the shelter, but that is not completely true. My father did come down to the city to see me on one occasion. I was stupid enough to think he just wanted to see how I was doing, but instead what he wanted to talk about was getting the name of whomever it was that got me pregnant and doing who knows what with the information. I remember him saying something about this boy having to take responsibility for his actions and he cannot get away with this. Understand, I had only two dates that past winter and they were both with the '59 Chevy. But I guess my father wanted to know for sure that that specific boy was the guilty one.

We were at a rather nice restaurant. I was sobbing uncontrollably because my father was really pushing me and pushing me. But for some reason I could not bring myself to say the boy's name out loud. It was not as if I felt the need to protect him, or anything like that. I do not know why I could not say his name, but I just could not. The fact that I could not stop crying did not help. So, when my father finally asked me if it was the '59 Chevy I just nodded my head. I can remember the waiter coming by the table on more than one occasion to see if we needed anything. Actually, I needed a rope and a kick stool, but I don't think they were on the menu. When we left the restaurant my father never apologized for upsetting me or asked how I was doing. He never even got out of the cab when it stopped at the shelter. He just told the cab driver to take him back to Grand Central. I spent the rest of the afternoon sitting on my bed crying. Thanks a lot, Dad.

CHAPTER FOUR

August 20th (my due date) was getting closer and closer. August 27th (my sister's wedding day) was getting closer and closer, too. If I delivered on the 20th, a Saturday, I would be out of the hospital by Thursday, the 25th. The plan was that we would go from New York City straight to Poughkeepsie so I could be fitted for my maid-of-honor dress, which would be picked up on Friday, in time for the wedding on Saturday. See, back then a five-day hospital stay was common for a normal delivery. Now childbirth is almost an out-patient procedure. I think the five-day plan makes more sense.

Anyway, by the morning of the 20th I was not in labor. Connie was two or three days past her due date and she, too, was kind of getting depressed. I was worried that I was going to miss my sister's wedding and then the whole town would know for sure what the reason was that I had been away for over four months. The concocted story was that I was going to a private school down in the city and that I had failed a couple of classes and had to go to summer school. But there was no way missing my sister's wedding could have been explained. Connie, on the other hand, was depressed because she just wanted the whole experience to be over so she could get back to Florida and get on with her life. She wanted it over and I, to be honest, wanted to stay pregnant forever and live in the shelter in New York City.

The secret entrance of the New York Foundling Hospital was just off the corner of 69th Street and Third Avenue. On the corner of 68th Street and Second Avenue was a drug store. Everyone staying at the shelter knew about the drug store because that was the place where you could sit at the counter and order a castor oil soda. It was believed that, if you were close to going into labor, the castor oil would help get you started. So, after lunch on Saturday, August 20th, Connie and I made a trip to the drug store. I ordered mine chocolate flavored. I recall that it was hard to get down, but we do what we have to do. I think both Connie and I expected to go into labor within the hour. When that did not happen, we were even more depressed and worried. She depressed . . . me worried.

I went to bed that night convinced that I would never give birth in time to make my sister's wedding. In the middle of the night, I woke up with diarrhea and just made it to the hall bathroom in time. The castor oil had given me a terrific stomachache, but no labor. Back in bed for a few more minutes and then up running to the bathroom again. On my third or fourth trip back from the bathroom I ran into Connie. She had the same problem. So instead of going back to bed we sat down on a bench in the hallway, both feeling sorry for ourselves. I remember saying to Connie, "That castor oil gave me such a stomachache, but it's better now. That stomachache is back. It is better now. I have got that stomachache again. At least it goes away." After about ten minutes of this Connie informed me that what I had was not a stomachache but, in fact, I was in labor. "Oh, no", I insisted. "It's just a stomachache . . . and here it comes again." I do not know how to explain this. I *knew* I was pregnant. I knew in order *not* to be pregnant any more I would have to go through labor. But I was in no way *prepared* for labor. There were no birth classes back then. We never got to talk to the girls who had already given birth because they never came back to the shelter afterwards. There were weekly doctor visits at the shelter, but we were never even informed about the different options we would have once we went into labor. It was 1960. I do not know if back then married women were having those conversations with their OB/GYN's. I just know that as unmarried teenagers we were all totally left in the dark. I was young enough so that none of my friends had ever given birth. It was not even talked about on television. When Lucy Ricardo went into labor, she walked into her living room in full hair and makeup saying something like, "Ricky, it's time." That was it. That was my preparation for what was in store.

Connie woke up Angela, the housemother on duty that night. She felt my belly for contractions and timed my "stomachaches" and informed me that I was in labor. Holy shit. So, at 2:00 a.m. on the morning of August 21, 1960, Connie walked me back to my room to help me get dressed. Angela got in touch with one of the nuns downstairs who would cover her shift at the shelter. Angela hailed a cab and we headed down to St. Vincent's hospital in the Village. The cab waited while she walked me into the hospital. She could not stay with me because she had to get back to the shelter. I have never felt so alone in my entire life. I remember the labor as being painful, but that is all I remember. I do not remember if or what kind of drugs I was given. I do not remember going from labor to delivery. I do not even remember the birth or being told that I had a girl. I do not remember there being nurses in the room, although I am sure they were there. I do remember asking the doctor his name. He said he was Doctor Cuts (or maybe he spelled it Kutz or some other way). But I remember asking him two or three times because I wanted to remember it. He was probably a med student or an intern or resident, not an obstetrician. For all I know he could have been a podiatrist or a dentist. I do not know why it was so important to me that I had to have his name. Maybe I thought that this was a turning point in my life, and I wanted to have all the details. Or maybe I *knew* it was a turning point in my life and I wanted to have all the details.

The girls from the shelter served out their five-day hospital stay in a six-bed room. Four beds lined up against a wall of windows separated by a nightstand. And one bed on either side of the door. I was surprised when I got to the room that there was only one other girl there that I knew. She was from the shelter and had given birth three or four days earlier. All the other girls/women were unwed mothers but had spent their pregnancy someplace else. One had her own apartment. One was living in a women's hotel. One was living with relatives. And one was living under the protection of some other charitable organization. Three of us were seeing our babies. The other three were not.

One of the other mothers was a beautiful redhead. A schoolteacher. If she had any baby weight to begin with, she had already lost it. She was so pretty. How could someone who seemed to have it all get herself into this situation? I was a teenager. I was stupid. But this woman was educated and beautiful and slender. I could not understand it. Another one of the mothers in the room was a pain in the ass. Before I was even settled in my bed, she made a point of coming over to me to tell me that, for medical reasons, she lost her virginity in a doctor's office. She had some weird problem whereby a doctor had to remove her hymen. And then a few years later she was at a party and had too much to drink and apparently some guy took advantage of her and it was the only time she ever had sex and got pregnant from that. It was important that everyone knew she was not a *virgin* when she had sex at the party because everyone knows you cannot get pregnant the first time you have sex. Okay, reader, you can stop laughing now. I swear, back then every boy who wanted to have sex with a virgin had to convince her that you cannot get pregnant the first time. As if the maidenhead works like a condom. Give me a break. But apparently it was super important to this girl that everyone she met knew she only had sex once and, more important, it was not her fault. She just had too much to drink. I do not give a shit. I just gave birth. Get away from my bed.

I can barely remember seeing my baby while I was in the hospital. It is not that I have blocked it. It is just that it was so long ago. I can remember some very specific details from back then, but I just don't remember much about those four days in the hospital. I do recall that when the babies were brought into the room so their mothers could feed them it was really awkward for the mothers that were not seeing their babies. One mother would go for a walk. I think the others dozed or read. I am not sure. No one breast fed so bottle feeding was the only time the babies were brought to the room. I had enough breast milk to feed an orphanage. My breasts were bound to help dry it up. I can remember standing in the shower and the milk, literally, pouring out of me like a fountain. What a waste. I can remember filling out the birth registry form. We were told that whatever names we gave our baby, the adopting family had to keep at least one, if not both. For that reason, some girls just gave their baby one name. But I named my daughter Maria Jayne. Maria after my favorite housemother at the shelter, someone I had known for only three months. What can I say? I had just turned seventeen and had a lot on my mind. It had never dawned on me to think about picking a name until after I gave birth. The middle name of Jayne was for my best friend Jane, but I liked spelling it the same way Jayne Mansfield spelled it. And just for an added reality check, under Father's Name on the birth form I was told I had to put *Unknown*. I couldn't just leave it blank? Great. So not only am I an unwed mother but unknown makes it sound like I am a slut, too. This is just great.

Under a normal schedule my five-day hospital stay would have had me discharged on Friday, August 26th. They did not count the day of delivery. But since I gave birth so early in the morning and the social worker knew my dilemma of having to be in my sister's wedding, she was able to get me discharged on Thursday. I remember that day. I remember almost every detail of that day. I had given birth on a Sunday but did not call home to tell my parents the news. I think it was Monday or Tuesday when one of them had called the shelter and only then found out that I had delivered. In the hospital the social worker informed me that my parents would be there to pick me up around noon on Thursday. "Swell", I thought. Why I could not just stay here in this hospital and never have to see them again and never have to go back home and never have to face anyone in that town.

But by Thursday morning I was ready to face the music. That was also the last time I would have a chance to see my daughter. I was sitting in one of the two lounge chairs in the room when the nurse brought her in around ten o'clock in the morning. I think now babies are transported in rolling bassinets, but back then the nurses just carried the babies in their arms. Someone in the nursery had taken the baby's hair and formed it into a little peak, like a little baby fauxhawk. When the nurse handed her to me, she said, "She's the pride of the nursery, she's so cute." And she *was* cute. She was 8 pounds, 5 ounces when she was born so she was a nice size. She was absolutely beautiful. And I knew I was seeing her for the last time. When the nurse came to take her back to the nursery, I can remember seeing the back of my daughter's head as the nurse walked away. That image is burned into my brain to this day.

At noon, my mother and sister walked into the hospital room. There were no hugs. There was no, "How are you doing?" Only, "Is this all your stuff?" I informed them that I had to go back to the shelter to get my belongings from there, at which point I was told that everything was already in the car. What??!! I never packed before I left in labor. There was no time. Well, apparently someone else took care of it. There was that shiver one gets when you realize someone has been touching your stuff. Oh, well. And then, just as we were leaving the room, a nurse that I did not recognize asked me if I had been seeing my baby. But I *thought* she had asked if I wanted my mother and sister to see my baby. So, I answered no to the question. I was not about to let them see this beautiful child. It would be their loss . . . my control. It was not until we were all at the front door that the nurse said directly to me that she thought I was one of the mothers who chose to see her baby and I told her that I was. She said she was curious then as to why, when I was leaving the floor, I told her I was not seeing my baby. I told her what I thought the question was and wondered if I could go back upstairs for one more look. But by then we were in the lobby and my father was there and, well, we had to get going. That is another thing I will never forgive myself for. The missed opportunity to have one more look.

CHAPTER FIVE

The two-hour ride back home from New York City was a lot of fun (sarcasm). My mother and sister talking about the wedding, and me staring out the car window. I felt different. I felt different the second I walked out of that hospital. Yes, I felt physically different. That is assumed. But I also felt mentally different or emotionally different. I felt so detached from my family. Like a stranger or a distant relative or a foreign exchange student. I felt as if I had been away from home for years and years and really had no connection to these people. I saw the three of them differently. Yes, I would have to spend the next year living in that house with my parents. My sister and soon-to-be brother-in-law would be living right across the street. But it was as if I were a boarder in the house. A boarder who spends most of her time in her room. A connection had been broken. Not that I ever felt all that close to any one of them before I got pregnant. My mother was cold. My father was hardly ever home. When he was not working, he was throwing down Bushmills at some local watering hole. (Feel free to read Suzanne Somers' bookkeeping *Secrets* if you want to see what it was like growing up with a functioning alcoholic father.) And my sister was this Pollyanna, perfect character with her own circle of friends. As teenagers I do not think we ever said more than ten words to each other on any given day. We did not dislike each other. We just were not close.

The minute we got home my mother and sister and I got in my mother's car and headed to Poughkeepsie for the fitting on my maid-of-honor dress. When you are fat you are always prepared for that humiliation when you attempt to put a garment on only to find out it is way too tight. But in this case my mother was smart enough to order a dress for me that was at least two sizes bigger than whatever I was wearing before I got pregnant. It was a good thing because not only was I twenty or thirty pounds heavier than I was before, but there had to be enough room for two or three layers of nursing pads. Those are the pads nursing mothers wear to avoid leaking milk through their clothes. And, man, was I leaking. There was no stopping it.

There was so much activity in the next forty-eight hours that I barely had time to think about what I had been through in the last nine months. There was the rehearsal and the dinner that followed. Seeing relatives that I had not seen in months. Being in the wedding itself just scared me to death. I felt like I was on stage. But I got through it and thought I could calm down at the reception. But (1) I was still leaking like crazy, and (2) who should show up uninvited but the '59 Chevy. Son of a bitch.

Here is the situation. Before I got pregnant, I would hang around with Gina. She was in my sister's grade (two years ahead of me) and one out of the crowd of ten girls that my sister hung out with. But because Gina failed history, she did not graduate with the rest of her class. So, in the fall of 1959 she had to go back to school every day for one hour to attend history class in the attempt to get her high school diploma. But that was all she did all day. She would drive her big, blue convertible to school; take the class; and then sometimes hang around afterwards and we would get lunch together at the local diner. I guess she picked me to hang with because she kind of knew me through my sister and (more important) I was no threat. No threat in the sense that if we went anyplace together all eyes would be on her and not the fat, ugly sidekick.

Anyway, before I ran away, Gina had been dating this guy named John. I thought they were rather tight. Gina was pretty and popular and had had a lot of boyfriends, but I got the impression this thing with John was more than just a high school romance. However, about two weeks before my due date my mother called me at the shelter just to check in with me and happened to mention that Gina was getting married. I remember I said, "To John?! That's great!" But my mother informed me that Gina would be marrying the '59 Chevy. How could that be? She was in love with John just three months ago. This could not be happening. Things do not change that fast. But, apparently, they do.

So, on August 20th, while I was sitting in a Second Avenue drug store in New York City drinking a castor oil soda, the father of my child was getting married. I can remember some of the other girls at the shelter telling me he did this because he thought it might keep him from being forced to marry me. But they did not get it. A forced marriage was never in the picture. That might have been a possibility if we had been dating for any length of time. But we had only had two dates. Barely past the rank of one-night-stand. In all the scenarios I had worked out in my head when I figured out that I was pregnant, getting married was never in the cards.

So, it is my sister's wedding reception. Gina and her cousin were two of my sister's bridesmaids. The band was playing. People were dancing. I was changing my nursing pads every half hour. And in walks the '59 Chevy. I think at a wedding it is assumed that the spouse of anyone in the wedding party is automatically invited. I do not know how that works. Are formal invitations sent out even though one member of the couple is a definite *yes*? Is the invitation extended verbally to the spouse or current significant other? All I know is the '59 Chevy and his bride of one week spent the rest of the reception making out in full view of everyone in attendance. Isn't that cute? They have only been married a week and can't keep their hands off each other. How precious? Isn't love grand? Now excuse me while I go change my nursing pads again.

Going back to school was only slightly anxiety provoking for me. I figured the first hour would be the worst and then I would just go through the motions for the next ten months until graduation. If I could survive what I had been through for the last nine months, then this would be a piece of cake. But first I had to register with the office before school opened. Remember, this was a very small high school. There was one woman who worked in the office. One woman did all the paperwork for the entire school. She was the receptionist, the typist, the secretary, the registrar, the social worker, the college advisor. She did it all. Granted, there were only 200 students in the entire high school. But, still, when I think back that this woman did everything required of her without even the aid of an electric typewriter, it boggles the mind.

So, anyway, my mother had to take me to school a few days before classes started. I can still remember the three of us sitting in this little office as this white-haired, prissy looking little woman wrote down the address of the office in New York where she would have to write to get a copy of my grades from my junior year . . . The Board of Education for the Physically Handicapped. I made up this cockamamie story about staying with a family friend down in the city and the girl who lived in the next apartment had broken her leg, so she had tutors come to her home to teach her, so they gave me permission to also finish up my junior year by taking classes with her. What do you think? Believable? I did not think so. But, what the hell. Let us just get this thing over with. My mother was squirming in her seat. I could tell she was mortified. On the ride home she reminded me, *again*, of how many lies she has had to tell because of what I did. Look what I was making her do. I was making her *lie*. God forbid.

I was somewhat nervous walking back into that high school on the first day of classes, but I can honestly say it was not traumatic. First of all, I just figured to hell with everyone. I do not owe these people an explanation. It was as if my whole attitude towards the world had changed when I walked out of that hospital in New York. And these little people with their little lives and their little town can just go to hell if they have a problem with where I was for the last five months. Piss on all of them. So, there I am, sitting in home room, waiting for the first bell, and these two boys came over to me. One of them pats my belly and says, "So what did you do with it?" with this big shit-eating grin on his face. I just shook my head as if in disbelief and said something like, "Oh, for Pete's sake. You guys. Get a life." And that was the end of it. That was it! No one ever said another word to me about where they thought I was for the last three months of the previous school year. Not one kid. Maybe they whispered about it behind my back. Do not know. Do not care. I just coasted through the rest of the day and the rest of the year.

There were a couple of situations that came up early that fall. One was having to take a day off school to go down to the city for my six-week postpartum checkup. It was done right at the shelter. One day a week the medical staff would come to the shelter and give routine check-ups to all the pregnant girls. They also did follow-up checkups to a handful of girls who, for whatever reason, did not want to use their own doctors, if they even had one. A lot of the mothers were from out of state, but a lot of the mothers who lived out of town lived far enough away that it would be an inconvenience to trek all the way back to New York for something that could have been done elsewhere. But my mother was not about to trust any OB/GYN with "the secret." So somewhere around the first of October we made the trip down to New York so that I could go through yet one more humiliating internal exam. I was glad that this would be the last time in my life I would ever have to have one of these things. (How stupid was I?)

It did feel strange going back to the shelter. I did not belong there. I had moved on (physically, not emotionally). I can remember seeing the housemother who had gone through the early part of labor with me. For a split second when I first saw her,

I got the impression that she had to remind herself of which one I was. There was definitely a hesitation. She recovered quickly enough, but how could she not remember sharing the most traumatic event in *my* life? It never occurred to me that my going into labor just may not have been the most traumatic event in *her* life. I brought pictures of my sister's wedding with me to show her, as if she cared. She pretended to be interested, but it was clinic day, and she was busy. I understood. I wanted her to take the time to sit down with me and ask me how things were going. How could she be so compassionate during my stay at the shelter and now, just because I was not living there anymore, show such a lack of interest in me? I had a lot of growing up to do, didn't I?

Another more upsetting situation that came up that fall was when I had to sign the final adoption papers. I knew it was coming. I was prepared. All I had to do was sign a paper. How hard is that? It was just a piece of paper. As it had been explained to me back at the shelter before I had given birth, the pre-adoption papers I signed while in the hospital were just an indication of intent. Whereas the final adoptions papers, for legal reasons, could not be signed for six weeks. That way the birth mother had time to evaluate the situation and be absolutely sure that these were her wishes. Fine. I understood that. I am completely on board with that. So, six weeks after birth would have been October 2nd, a Sunday. Okay, so since these papers cannot be signed *before* the six weeks (or they would not be legal) then I assumed I would be taking care of this on October 3rd or shortly thereafter. So, for that reason, when one day during the last week of September, my mother told me she would be picking me up after school and we would be driving to Poughkeepsie to the Catholic Charities office so I could sign the papers, I was shocked. How could this be? It has not been six weeks yet! They told me I would have to wait six weeks in order for the papers to be legal! I still have a few more days! They cannot do this to me! Stop! I guess you could say I was not as prepared to sign these papers as I thought I was. My mother was thrilled to get this over with. I am guessing she felt like until I actually signed those papers, I could still change my mind. I had no intention of changing my mind. But she did not know that because we never talked about it. In fact, we never talked about much of anything. Going through the motions. Going through the motions.

I sat in the Catholic Charities office and signed the papers. I did not read them. I think the man behind the desk might have explained them to me. I do not know. Just . . . where do I sign. I wanted to say something about it not being a full six weeks yet, but I did not feel like I had much of a say in the matter. Adults were making these decisions for me. I just had to go along. So, I signed my name. And then the waterworks started. I do not know why. I did not know why then, and I do not know why now. Maybe it is because it was so final. I knew there was no way I could raise a child. I knew I was doing the best thing. I knew I was turning my baby over to a loving family who really wanted a child. I just think I was crying because I felt sorry for myself. Or maybe it was because I had been holding it in for six weeks. Or maybe it was because there was nobody there to give me a hug and comfort me. Oh, did I mention that my mother was in the room with me when I signed the papers? Like I said, there was nobody there to give me a hug.

After the paperwork was taken care of, I was told to sit in the waiting room while my mother stayed in the office behind closed doors. I did not care what they were discussing. I just wanted to get out of there. On the way home my mother told me that the Catholic Charities man had called the shelter in New York and had spoken to the nun in charge to tell her that the papers were signed. She asked to talk to my mother to see how I was doing. I have no idea what my mother told her. But what surprised me was my mother told me she asked the nun if I had a boy or a girl. She told me the nun said, "You mean Barbara didn't tell you?" My mother told me she told the nun that, not only had I not told her, but that I did not want to talk about it. Really, mother? Really? *I am* the one who does not want to talk about it?

How about *you are* the one who does not want to talk about it EVER AGAIN? I wanted to jump out of the car and just fly away. I wanted to disappear. I wanted to run away. Damn. I keep forgetting. I tried that already.

Just one other thing about that visit to Catholic Charities in Poughkeepsie. When my mother talked on the phone, she told the nun that I had a letter ready to mail that I had written to Connie. Connie had given me her address in Florida before I left the shelter and we promised to keep in touch. I did not give her my address because I was not exactly sure what life back in hell was going to be like. Would my mother be reading all my mail? Would I even be allowed to have mail? So, between the wedding and getting back in the swing of school, it had taken me six weeks to get a letter written to Connie. But my mother said the nun told her that they strongly discourage the girls in the shelter from keeping in touch after they leave. Different girls have different levels of secrecy and it was just not a good idea to have someone in a position where they might have to explain a friendship somewhere down the road. Or running the risk of having someone in a position to reveal a secret someone else was trying to keep.

So, my mother told me I could not mail the letter and I was not allowed to keep in touch with someone from "that place." So, I tore the letter up. I felt really bad about it. I felt that Connie would think that the minute I left the shelter that I completely forgot about her. Nothing could have been further from the truth. It was Connie who actually got me through the three-plus months that I spent there. We shared so much. Not just the castor oil sodas and me going through labor. We bonded in a way that only two scared, pregnant, unwed mothers living in a shelter could. We listened to each other's stories and fears and hopes and questions. It was a hard time for both of us for different reasons. I wanted to know how her whole birthing experience was. I wanted to know what life was like back home. I just wanted her to know that if she ever felt like talking (writing) about anything, that I would be there for her. But I never got a chance to tell her. So, Connie, if for some crazy reason you are reading this, I am sorry. I am sorry I never got to thank you for being a friend.

CHAPTER SIX

For as long as I could remember back then I wanted to be a teacher. Specifically, a math teacher. I think I liked mathematics because there was no judgment. The answer was either right or wrong. No one could question your essay writing skills. There were no dates and names to memorize. To me (back then) numbers were exciting. I had visions of myself teaching to a roomful of bored, disinterested teenagers, and the joy of watching the facial expressions as each and every one of them came around and fell in love with algebra and trigonometry and (my favorite) geometry. Not only was I going to be a brilliant teacher, but the students were going to love me because I was going to be really cool.

However, there were no counselors at my high school. At the beginning of the senior year those students who were planning to go on to college were given forms to fill out to apply to take the SAT"s, but that was about it. And when I did take the SAT, as I expected, my math score was kind of high and my English score was kind of low. I applied to a dozen colleges in New York State, but after receiving eleven rejection letters I gradually gave up the dream of becoming this world-renowned math teacher. The one acceptance letter came from Fredonia State University out near Buffalo. I don't know why I didn't go there. Maybe by the time the letter came I already felt defeated.

So, if not college, then what? I knew I never, never, ever wanted to work in an office. Ever! To me that would be the most pathetic thing a person could do. By the time I was a senior my sister was a civil servant, and I would visit her office and feel depressed for hours after I left. Those boring people doing their boring jobs at those ugly desks with all those ugly piles of paper. Day after day after day. How miserable of an existence is that? No, I was never going to go down that path. So, if not college and not office work, then what? Remember Jane's cousin, Dorothy, the girl who took me to her family doctor in Yonkers? She had a job in a factory. A ballpoint pen factory. She sat on a stool all day and screwed caps on ballpoint pens. What a great job, I thought. I could do that. So, after graduation the search began to find a factory job in Poughkeepsie.

Through a friend of a friend of a family friend I was able to land a job at Western Printing and Lithographing, Inc. They made comic books. Comic books and picture books and paperback books. This was going to be great. The hours were six-thirty in the morning until two-thirty in the afternoon. Women started at something like $1.58 an hour and men started at $1.72 an hour. That is just the way it was . . . get over it. The minimum wage back then was a dollar an hour, so to be making over fifty percent above that seemed like a lot. And it was a lot. Gas was only thirty-five cents a gallon, so that kind of puts it in perspective. My father had given me a car for graduation. I figured I would drive to work and do my thing during the week and have my weekends without a care in the world. Not like my sister who would worry all weekend about the stuff she left on her desk that would still be there on Monday morning. I would be really lucky to be working in a factory.

There was just one little problem. The job was hell. Absolute, pure, unadulterated hell. Because I got the job through a friend of a friend of a family friend, I was not fired on the first day. My first assignment was to wrap comic books in heavy, brown paper. Sounds simple enough, I know. Try to picture this . .

. I stood at a two-foot by two-foot waist-high table. There was a conveyor belt immediately on my left, and a set of thin shelves on my right. Each shelf held a supply of various sizes of paper. I was instructed to use a different size depending on the number of comic books in each stack coming down the conveyor belt. There were stacks of only six books and stacks of one hundred books and every size in between. As the stacks came down the belt the object was to eyeball them and then grab the correct size sheet of paper from the shelving and place one of those pieces of paper on the worktable. There would be a label sitting on top of the pile of books. So as the belt continued to move, I would lift the label off the pile and place it off to the side. Then lift the pile of comic books over onto the brown paper I had selected. Wrap the pile and tuck each end of the paper so it formed a nice, neat bundle. Put the label back on top of the now wrapped stack and place it back on the conveyor belt where it would be sent down the line to women who would bind these bundles in wire and glue the label to the top.

The only problem was that the stacks of comic books were coming down the conveyor belt faster than I could wrap them. So, I learned (this is genius) that while the *large* stacks would not fit in the smaller paper, *any* size stack would fit in the largest paper. So rather than waste precious seconds trying to figure out what size paper to use and then pulling that paper off the shelf, I took *all* the large paper, placed it on the work surface in front of me, thus saving two steps in this ten-step operation. The only problem with *this* brilliant plan of mine was that, when trying to wrap six comic books in a piece of paper that was designed to wrap a hundred comic books, there was quite a bit of extra paper left over and it made for these giant flaps and folds and . . . well . . . there was a reason why they used different size paper. So, five minutes after I would send one of these origami creations down the belt I would hear, "Someone up there is using the wrong size paper!!!!" I lasted one day on that assignment.

On my second day I was assigned to stacking pallets.

There is an order to it. A pattern must be followed so that the final stack does not end up being heavier on one side. When the pallet was stacked with bundles of comic books, it must look like a neat box. Then someone with a forklift will take these neatly stacked pallets away. I knew the pattern. I was all set. There was just one tiny problem. I was stacking the piles of comic books on the wrong sized pallets. My neat, perfectly formed, box-shaped stack hung out over all four sides by about six inches. I did not even know this was a problem. They looked good to me. However, just before lunch, when the forklift driver came to pick up my pallets, this overhang was pointed out to my supervisor. I spent the afternoon undoing and redoing all the work I had done that morning.

On my third day I was sent to help in an area that made large coffee-table books. The machine I was assigned to was used to stamp the title of the book onto the spine. There would be a stack of flat book covers piled up. A suction arm would pick up one cover at a time and place it on a flat surface. A printer would come down and stamp the spine. And then another suction arm would pick that cover up and move it away. However, as it turned out, when the first suction arm pulled one cover off the stack, the corner of the cover would scrape along the next cover, leaving a very noticeable mark on the surface. You cannot have something like that on an expensive book. So, my first job this day was to put a piece of heavy brown paper in between each cover so, as the machine pulled the top cover away, the corner would scrape the paper and not the next cover. Simple enough. I spent the entire morning putting paper between stacks and stacks of covers. Then, after lunch I loaded the first stack of covers, about fifty, onto the printing machine. As the suction arm pulled the first cover away, my job then was to take out the paper so that when the suction arm came back it would take hold of the next cover and not the paper. There was just one tiny problem. Actually, there were two tiny problems. Number one: nobody told me how incredibly fast this machine functioned. And number two: once I had a piece of paper in my right hand and a piece of paper in my left hand, what would I use to grab the next piece of paper? It was not a pretty sight. Brown paper flying all over the place. Book covers shooting across the room as the suction machine grabbed half cover and half paper. Machine operator screaming. Me crying. Not a good day.

The fourth day I was dispensed to the department that made paperback books. Specifically, these little books about birds. My assignment there could not have been easier. There was no heavy brown paper involved. No suction machines. No wooden pallets. All I had to do was pick up three books as they came down the conveyor; have two facing in one direction and the center book facing in the opposite direction; wrap a piece of pre-adhesive tape around them; and put them back on the conveyor. I know what you are thinking. As soon as you read the word "conveyor" you think of that famous *I Love Lucy* scene with the chocolates. And while that was an amusing scene, no doubt, at least Lucy could put some of the chocolate in her mouth and under her hat and down her dress. However, when you are the last person on a conveyor belt and you are told not to let any un-taped books go past you, it is a completely different situation. Again, I misjudged how fast the belt would run and the fact that the women at the other end were throwing down bird books like a Las Vegas blackjack dealer. Rather than let the books go by me, I would have to grab them and stack them around my work area waiting for a lull so that I could get caught up. You guessed it. There was no lull. Within minutes I had a wall of books around me that looked like an Apache fort.

As I drove home at the end of each day it became clear to me that perhaps, just perhaps, I was not cut out for factory work. But if not factory work and not office work and not college, then what? In my second week there I was transferred from department to department with even less success than I had during my first week. But towards the end of that second week one of the foremen walked up to me and asked if I knew how to type. I had to tell him no but asked why the question. He informed me that there was an opening in the office, and they wanted to know if I were interested, but it required typing. SON OF A BITCH!!!!! Out of a hundred women working in this factory he asked _me_ if I could type? Why did I not take typing in high school? Why? Why? Why? Stupid. Stupid. Stupid. There was this golden opportunity. The chance of a lifetime. The one job I always said I would never do, and here I was crying all the way home because I missed out on the opportunity of a lifetime. I might just point out, though, that I was not _exactly_ chosen at random to be offered the office job. The friend of a friend of a family friend that had helped me get the job in the first place apparently had put in a word for me to see if they could get me out of the factory and into the office as soon as an opportunity came up. All that help and I was not able to take advantage of it.

I told my parents of this missed, golden opportunity and how I, who never, ever wanted to work in an office, was so upset because I lacked any office skills. They both suggested I go to secretarial school. Just the word "school" was upsetting, but what other choice did I have? So, on a Saturday in late August the three of us made our way down to White Plains and Berkeley Secretarial School to see about the program and if there were any openings for that fall. I was enrolled on the spot. The school gave us the names of a couple of local families that took students in as boarders. We checked them out and picked the nicest looking one. The next Monday I gave my three-day notice to the comic book factory. They were extremely upset to lose such an outstanding worker, I am sure. Then, during the first week of September in 1961, I got my introduction to a-s-d-f, space.

CHAPTER SEVEN

Once I had accepted the fact that I was going to end up working in an office and needed to learn the skills for this death sentence, I actually enjoyed secretarial school. In fact, I had a blast for the next ten months. I made friends with a few girls that were also brought to the school kicking and screaming. These were not like the other two girls that were also boarders at the same house where I was staying. No . . . those two were serious, focused, wholesome girls who dd not smoke or drink and were both engaged to boys back home. The girls I ended up hanging with were all smokers, never missed an opportunity to imbibe, and liked the boys. I do not know what White Plains is like now, but from September of 1961 to June of 1962 every Thursday night was party night. At school we had to dress in someone's preconceived fantasy of what secretaries were supposed to look like. That meant heels and stockings and proper business attire every day. So, by Thursday night we were so happy to get out of this uniform that we changed our clothes and our personalities, and all piled into some big old car that one of the girls owned and hit half the bars in the city. Nobody knew "my secret." Nobody knew I grew up never being part of the "in" crowd. High school was over and done and a million years in the past. I could feel my life taking a turn. I was growing up and it felt good.

As much as I enjoyed the year at secretarial school, I had

to accept the fact that it was time to head to the city and go job hunting. There were a few girls in the school who got jobs in the White Plains area, but most of them, me included, knew from day one that we were going to be working in New York. The school set up appointments, so I dressed up in my best navy-blue suit and went on interviews. I first went to New York University, then Union Carbide, and finally Remington Rand. The NYU location where I was interviewed was their Washington Square campus. The Village. THE VILLAGE!!!! GREENWICH VILLAGE!!!! I *had* to get this job. I did not care what I would be doing. All I knew was that absolutely nothing would be cooler than living and working in Greenwich Village.

I passed NYU's typing test at that first interview but could not master the shorthand test. The man who interviewed me was so kind. He told me I was probably nervous because this was my first interview. He suggested I come back in a week and try the test again. I went on to the Union Carbide and Remington Rand interviews, passed all their tests, and was offered a job at both places paying over twenty dollars a week higher than NYU was offering. But it was not enough to lure me away from Greenwich Village. So, a week after my first interview at the university I went back and nailed the shorthand test. I was sent to the department that taught English as a second language to meet the office manager there. Most people who worked in the offices at the university were just doing it for the free tuition. I am guessing it's still like that. But I had no ambition to go to college. I just wanted an office job by day and The Village to explore on nights and weekends. I pictured myself sitting in coffee houses, listening to a beatnik reciting poetry, while another beatnik sat cross-legged on the floor, playing bongos. Now I ask you, what could be cooler than that?

No one ever got rich working for a University. That is not why people do it. People go to work at a university because they love to teach, or because they have educated themselves into a corner, or they think that's all they can do with their degree(s).

People go to work in university *offices* for the free tuition, period. Why would anyone take an office job for twenty-five percent less than they could make if they went to work for a profit-making company? Well, there is that Greenwich Village cool factor.

So, in the fall of 1962 I found a little one-room apartment on Waverly Place, a block from my office and a block from Washington Square Park. It was categorized as one-and-one-half rooms. I never did find that half room. The walls were painted this awful shade of dark avocado (but I did not care). The bathroom had a purple sink, tub and toilet and the tiles were black. If you stood at the sink the toilet hit the back of your knees (but I did not care). The kitchen was part of the living room and consisted of a sink; a two-foot-high refrigerator; and a hot plate that would not even boil water (but I did not care). There were two windows that faced an air shaft, *but* if I cranked them open all the way and leaned way out and cranked my neck all the way to the right, I could see the top of the Empire State Building. Cool, right?

The apartment came furnished. Make that, the apartment came "furnished" with a day bed that had to be twenty-five years old; a little round table and two chairs; a small desk; and a side chair, also twenty-five years old (but I did not care). There was a telephone with no dial on it because all calls went through a switchboard down on the ground floor. There was an elevator, but it was not self-service. The old men who operated the switchboard also ran the elevator. So, if you wanted to make a call while the guy was taking someone up to the fourteenth floor, you had to wait for him to go up and come back down. And, likewise, if you needed the elevator and the guy was trying to handle more than one call, you had to wait (but I did not care). At night, the front door to the building would be locked, so if you got home too late you could stand out in the freezing cold forever waiting for the switchboard/elevator operator to show up. But I did not care because I had my own apartment. My *own* apartment.

My rent was $125 a month, which was way too high for

someone who brought home $105 every two weeks. But stuff was really cheap back then. A subway ride was only fifteen cents. Cigarettes were something like fifty cents a pack. You could go to Chock Full O' Nuts and get coffee, a sandwich and a brownie for less than a dollar. A Twofer coupon (for two theater tickets) were only fifteen dollars so all you needed was seven fifty and a friend to see anything on Broadway, and I did. All utilities were included in my rent so there was no utility bill or cable TV bill. I did have to pay twenty cents for every phone call I made, but there were no message units. (That was a system back then in New York where you had to pay for the length of each call you made. It may still be like that. I do not know.)

I settled into learning about life in academia and learning how to do all the things in an office that I was never taught in secretarial school. There were enough young, single people working in the office so there was always someone to go to dinner with or to go have a drink with. When I read Frank McCourt's book, *Tis*, I remember him mentioning going to Rocky's Bar when he worked at NYU. Rocky's was, maybe, two hundred feet from the front door of my apartment building. I, too, contributed to help Rocky pay his overhead. I wonder if it is still there.

Meanwhile, the Cuban missile crisis was making news; Lincoln Center opened; Johnny Carson started hosting The Tonight Show; the Beatles started recording; *Who's Afraid of Virginia Wolf* opened on Broadway; Richard Nixon told us we would not have him to kick around anymore; The Four Seasons were telling us that big girls did not cry; and James Meredith started classes at the University of Mississippi.

In 1963, unable to afford my rent on my meager take-home pay, I moved to a slum on Second Street, between Avenues A and B. Third floor walk-up. Bathtub in the kitchen. Overrun by cockroaches and mice. But the rent was $54 a month as compared to $125 for the Waverly Place apartment. My take-home pay was still just above $100 every two weeks. To supplement my income, I would bring back a week's supply of groceries every time I took the train to my parent's place on the weekends. And there were usually a few extra dollars in overtime every month. But it was still tight. I hired an exterminator and got rid of the bugs and rodents (I did not know that was the landlord's job), but I never really felt safe in that apartment or walking on Second Street late at night. But for $54 a month, including utilities, I had to toughen up and make the best of it.

Meanwhile, the 747 jumbo jet was introduced; the PanAm Building opened on top of Grand Central Station; Alcatraz closed; Pop Art hit the art world; Timothy Leary was fired for supplying his students with LSD; the Russians put a woman in space; ZIP codes were initiated; Martin Luther King, Jr. told us he had a dream; the Washington-Moscow hot line went into effect; Valium, audio cassettes and lava lamps came onto the market; The Chiffons were singing about how fine he was; and President John Fitzgerald Kennedy was assassinated.

In 1964 I had had enough of living in a slum. I was ashamed to have anyone see the place, friend or date. There was a fire in the building next to mine, which showed me how a smoldering cigarette could destroy everything in one of these tinder boxes. Plus, my apartment had been burglarized twice. Both times, because I was afraid to spend the night in the place after the break in, I called my friend Jane and took the subway and bus in the middle of the night to her apartment in Yonkers. By then she was married with two young boys. While sitting in her kitchen the morning after my second burglary her father just happened to call. She said to him, "Guess who's here because she got robbed again?" His immediate response was that I had to get out of that apartment, and he was going to do something about it.

As luck would have it, Jane's father was working for the Mitchell Lama Housing Program, which managed middle-income co-ops throughout the city. There just happened to be a development almost ready for occupancy located on First Avenue that ran between 2nd and 6th Streets. The development had had a number of cancellations, so a few apartments were still available.

The next day he took me to two different one-bedroom apartments so I could pick which view I wanted. My choices were a view of the East River or a view of the Empire State Building. I instantly fell in love with all the buildings looking uptown. The apartment I chose was on the sixteenth floor. Other than the co-op buildings, all the other buildings in the neighborhood were only five stories high, making for the most spectacular uninterrupted uptown view. (I would absolutely love to go back to that apartment and have one more look at that view, but I doubt the present residents would go for it. Can you imagine some old lady knocking on your door and asking to look out your window?)

I did not have the $2,000 required to purchase shares in the corporation so I had to borrow it from my parents. But my rent, or rather monthly maintenance as they called it, was income-based and less than $100 a month. I could swing that. So, in early 1964 I moved into apartment 16E at 60 First Avenue. To celebrate I treated myself to a trip to London and Paris. Notice, I did not have the money to buy my co-op shares, but I managed to come up with the money to go to Europe. Priorities. Priorities.

Meanwhile, the Beatles invaded America; Lyndon Johnson declared war on poverty; the Surgeon General suggested that cigarette smoking *may* possibly be hazardous to our health; Cassius Clay became the heavy-weight champion; Ford introduced the Mustang; Kitty Genovese was murdered; Jack Ruby was found guilty; Jeopardy debuted; The World's Fair opened in New York; The Warren Commission released their report; Lenny Bruce was convicted of obscenity; The Shangri-las were singing about the leader of the pack; and the United States' involvement in Vietnam was escalating.

In 1965, having been browbeaten by every teacher at the department where I worked at NYU, I started taking some night classes to work towards a bachelor's degree. I had no idea what path to follow so it was suggested that I start with NYU's School of Commerce. I worked in an office. These were business courses. I guess it made as much sense as anything else. I did not want to go back to school. I hated it. I hated sitting in the classroom. I hated doing the work required. I hated the weight of term papers hanging over my head all the time. I was a terrible student. I was taking two classes and received a C and a D, which is a GPA of 1.5, which is low enough to be put on academic probation. What an embarrassment. Here I was, surrounded by all these educated people every day, and I could not even manage an entry-level business class. How stupid am I?

Meanwhile, Malcolm X was assassinated; there were riots in Selma and Watts; Bob Dylan went electric; Richard Hickock and Perry Smith were hanged; Sandy Koufax threw a perfect game; Willie Mays joined the 500 club; the St. Louis arch was completed; the World's Fair closed; The McCoys were asking Sloopy to hang on; all kinds of stuff were happening in space; and the war in Vietnam was escalating.

In 1966 someone told me that the Women's House of Detention was looking for volunteers. Back then the building was just off Sixth Avenue in the west village. The top floors of the building were for women who had been convicted of a crime and were serving their time, while the bottom floors were for girls that could not afford bail and were waiting to go to trial. The name of the volunteer organization was the Friendly Visitors. They performed a variety of services, but their main purpose was to visit girls that had no family in the area and, therefore, no visitors.

The office I worked in at NYU was open until 10:00 p.m., so on Tuesdays it was my turn to work the late shift, leaving my mornings free to do my volunteer work. I was assigned a young girl from out of state who had asked to have a volunteer visitor. I do not remember what she was in for. Most of the girls were arrested for prostitution; but, as I recall, this girl was there for something else. I met her in one of the visitor's booths. I introduced myself and gave her a pack of cigarettes (a little present from the Friendly Visitors). She was probably the only girl in the whole building that did not smoke. Within a minute of our meeting, she started crying and telling me all her problems. She told me about all the mean things the other inmates would do to her because she was naïve and immature. She told me about all these physical problems she had that the staff would not even address. And the whole time she was sobbing all I could think of was, "What the *hell* am I doing here?" In no way was I prepared to handle this. After our first visit I spoke with one of the Friendly Visitor officials and was basically told not to pay too much attention to what the girl was saying, but just to be there for her to have someone to talk to. But after two or three more visits I knew I was not even equipped to be a sounding board. I had to pass her off to another volunteer.

Meanwhile, Indira Gandhi was elected Prime Minister of India; John Lennon declared the Beatles more popular than Jesus; LSD was declared illegal; The Zodiac Killer killed his first victim; Nancy Sinatra was singing about her boots; all kinds of stuff was happening in space; and the war in Vietnam was escalating even more.

In 1967, still a volunteer at the women's prison, I switched over to helping a woman who taught a ceramics class on Saturdays. We had a good routine. She would show me how to start a particular project, and then when the girls arrived for the class, I would show them what I had learned. They had no idea I had learned the technique only fifteen minutes earlier. It was really rewarding watching these girls discover their own talents. Most, if not all of them, had never had an opportunity to be creative. To survive at the house of detention they had to be tough or at least act tough. But in the ceramics class they could let their guard down. These girls were barely older than I was and yet they had lived such traumatic lives. Drug addiction; prostitution; abuse. The saddest thing to learn in talking to them was that when their sentence was up, they had nothing to go back to except the life that led them to the jail in the first place. I was developing an interest in their world and changed my major from business to social work. Besides my night classes at NYU, I enrolled in a program co-sponsored by the New York City

Department of Correction, the Postgraduate Center for Mental Health, and the United States Department of Justice.

The program was called In-Service Training Program in Narcotic Addiction. It involved going to Ryker's Island prison every other week to listen to a lecture and then meet in small groups to discuss the lecture. The group I was in was headed by a psychologist and included correction officers and social workers and school counselors and me, an office worker. Between interacting with the girls at the jail and lectures and discussions at Ryker's Island, I learned so much about the sad, sad world that addicts lived in. I had no idea what I was going to do with this information. I just knew I wanted to work in some related field and figured if I just kept plugging away towards the bachelor's degree, that somewhere along the line something would click, and I would have a goal or a focus.

As a volunteer at the woman's jail, I also helped with a few other activities. I helped distribute Christmas presents (a real eye-opener when we stopped at the solitary confinement wing). But the best activity was a fund raiser which involved getting some rather wealthy residents of Greenwich Village to open up their apartments for a Saturday afternoon tour. People paid five dollars to walk around the village and stop at seven or eight apartments to look inside and see how they were decorated. There was a penthouse on Sixth Avenue, a converted stable in Washington Mews, and everything in between. I stood at the entrance at one of these apartments and checked tickets, but towards the end of the day I was allowed to go take the tour myself. It was nice to see the way people with money live. I wanted to go home and set fire to my own furniture. But I will tell you, except for the Sixth Avenue penthouse, none of these apartments had a view that could even compare to mine.

Meanwhile, the first Super Bowl game was played; Stalin's daughter defected to the United States: Israel had a six-day war; Expo '67 opened in Montreal; Muhammad Ali was stripped of his title; Elvis got married; Mickey Mantle joined the 500 club; Sgt.

Pepper's *Lonely Hearts Club Band* was released; *Hair* opened on Broadway; Christian Barnard performed a heart transplant; there were riots in Newark; Aretha Franklin was asking us to respect her; all kinds of stuff was happening in space; and the war in Vietnam was getting even worse.

CHAPTER EIGHT

By 1968 it dawned on me that, if I stayed at NYU, I was never going to be anything more than a clerk. I was working for a university, but I did not have a college degree. Formal education was the way worth was measured. But taking only two courses a semester meant getting my bachelor's was years away. I got fed up one day and just quit. I gave my boss a two-week notice and then signed up with a bunch of temporary agencies. There were no shortages of jobs for temp workers back then. I could pick the days I wanted to work, and I could pick the location, too. I lived on First Avenue so I knew I did not want to work on the west side or downtown in the financial district because that would involve a bothersome commute. So, when there was an opening at the Ford Foundation, located just off First Avenue at 42nd Street, I took the assignment.

The location was great, half a block from the United Nations. Just steps away from all kinds of shops and restaurants. Within a couple of months, I was hired by the foundation. The department I worked in was nice enough to let me take off every other Tuesday afternoon to continue with the Ryker's Island lectures. No longer employed by NYU, I had to withdraw from the night classes there. That was the most rewarding part of changing jobs. No more term papers or reading those horribly boring textbooks. I was free. Life was good.

Meanwhile, Rowan and Martin's Laugh-in debuted; North Korea seized the USS Pueblo: Bowie Kuhn became the baseball commissioner; the 911 emergency phone system went into service; Martin Luther King, Jr. and Robert Kennedy were assassinated; Hank Aaron joined the 500 club; Hollywood adopted the movie rating system; Jacqueline Kennedy became Jackie O; the Beatles released their white album; Marvin Gaye was telling us about what he heard through the grape vine; all kinds of stuff continued to happen in space; and the war in Vietnam was getting out of control.

By 1969 I had started taking night classes at John Jay College of Criminal Justice, part of the City University of New York. For some reason, my attitude towards higher education had changed and I actually looked forward to going back to school. The fact that the student population of John Jay was ninety percent male had absolutely nothing to do with it. My fellow students were mostly cops and correction officers. Most nights, not only would I be the only female in class, but I would also be the only one sitting in class that was not wearing a gun. Mind you, I still had no specific goal. Just plugging away at classes. My declared major was Correction Administration, but I had no idea what I was going to do with a degree in that field with absolutely no experience. Teaching ceramics and distributing Christmas presents at a woman's prison hardly counts as "experience."

At the suggestion of a retired policeman, I took the NYC police officer's exam. I scored 95 on the written portion and passed the eye exam but failed the test for physical strength because I could not do a sit-up while holding a barbell behind my neck. That was a sad, sad day. The exam was given only once every four years and by the time it came around again, I would be over the maximum age limit to take it. Learning how to do the kind of sit-up that was required simply requires practice. I blamed myself for not doing my homework to find out what was needed to pass that one physical test. I ran the obstacle course in the allotted time and was able to lift a barbell over my head and hold it there. It was just that stupid sit-up that did me in. I have thought about that situation many, many times over the years and have often wondered how different my life could have been if I had been able to join New York City's police force rather than spend the rest of my life working in an office. Oh, well.

Meanwhile, Yasser Arafat became the leader of the PLO; Golda Meir became Prime Minister of Israel; Muammar Gaddafi became the ruler of Lybia; Charles de Gaulle resigned; John Lennon and Yoko Ono got married; Hee Haw debuted; the Woodstock Music and Arts Festival took place; Peter, Paul and Mary were taking an airplane ride; Neil Armstrong walked on the moon; and things were falling apart in Vietnam.

In 1970 a co-worker spotted a tiny little ad in the New York Daily News. It said something about the Auxiliary Police of the City of New York looking for new recruits. There would be weekly classes followed by a written exam. Hey. It could not hurt to check into it. What did I have to lose? The classes were given at the Central Park Precinct. As I remember the location there was a small collection of old buildings. An old brick or stone building that held the few offices. There was a shooting range there. The precinct had a mounted unit, but I do not recall if there were stables there, or if the horses were kept at another location. There were twenty or thirty of us in attendance every week at the classes. I was the only female. At the end of the training, I passed the test with flying colors. I never once had to do a sit-up. So, every Wednesday after work at the Ford Foundation I would make my way up to the Central Park station house and do whatever paperwork had been saved for me. I always felt good about my time with the auxiliary police. I felt that the time I spent doing paperwork in the precinct office helped in some tiny way with the city's serious crime problem. I felt as if it freed up a regular policeman to get out from behind a desk and get out on the streets where he was needed. Oh, and did I mention that back then the Central Park Precinct had no female officers? Plus, there was that mounted unit. Gotta love those uniforms. (Sigh!)

Meanwhile, All My Children debuted; Expo '70 opened in Osaka; Apollo 13 made it back to earth; Four students were killed at Kent State; Ernie Banks joined the 500 Club; the Ford Pinto was introduced; the first New York City marathon was held; Monday Night Football premiered; Mango Jerry let us know how great the summertime was; and there were nation-wide protests against the war in Vietnam.

In 1971, still working for The Ford Foundation, I made a trip to Africa. The foundation had so many field offices all over the world and just dealing with the people at those locations was enough to give a person wanderlust. So, I mapped out a trip that had me stopping in Casablanca, Lagos, Nairobi, and Addis Ababa, with plane changes in Khartoum and Cairo. I spent three days in Casablanca and a week each in Nairobi and Addis. It was wonderful. Wonderful! I spent a day with my counterpart in the Nairobi field office, but other than that it was all vacation. Casablanca was strange and exotic. Men wearing djellabas. The casbah. Looking out my hotel window in the morning and seeing carts filled with fruits and vegetables being pulled by donkeys. Everything was different. Lagos was busy and confusing. Lots of traffic. Everyone seemed as if they were in a hurry. I have heard people make that same comment about New York City, but I was used to the pace in New York. Lagos was a different pace. I felt like I was in the way.

Nairobi, as I remember it, was a beautiful, clean city. Yes, there was lots of traffic, but as I recall it did not have the chaotic feel that Lagos had. While in Kenya I spent a night at the Treetops Inn. A rather rustic structure constructed on the top of . . . what else . . . tree trunks, where I was able to sit on the balcony, drinking a gin and tonic, and watch elephants and rhinos walk up to a watering hole for a drink. I felt as if I were at the coolest place on earth. It was a far cry from Rocky's basement on Waverly Place. Yes, indeed.

Addis Ababa was quite an eye opener. Haile Selassie was emperor at the time. I can remember walking on the street around his palace and seeing some of his collection of lions in their cages. To my right was the back of the palace and to my left were slums the likes of which I could never have imagined. A small boy, not more than four or five, came running after me and walked along side of me and kept asking for money. It was over forty years ago, but I can still remember how yellow the whites of his eyes were. There was nobody else on the street except the two of us. I can remember thinking if I reach into my purse to pull out a dollar, will ten other boys come running out of the slums and want their share. I had to turn him down. I just did not feel safe. On a much busier street a lot of Ethiopians had made their way to the city to see the golden statue of the Lion of Judah. Apparently, it had been captured by the Italians over thirty years before and had just made its way back to its original homeland. It was quite impressive, but I am sure it meant more to the Ethiopians than it did to me.

I remember the marketplace in Addis. It would probably compare to a farmer's market here in the states . . . but a farmer's market from a hundred years ago. There was a woman squatting on a table and scooping out handfuls of butter from a giant wooden vat. She would shape the butter into a ball and wrap it in newspaper. That was how she sold it. A man was selling honey that was contained in something that looked like a giant burlap bag. Apparently back in 1971 they were not aware that burlap did not hold honey all that well, as evidenced by how much of it was oozing out all over the bag. I do not know how much the honey was going for, but I'm guessing the thousands of flies that accompanied each bag were included in the price.

I was scheduled to fly home from Addis, with a plane change in Rome. But PanAm notified me that there would be a slight schedule change. I would fly Ethiopian Airlines to Athens, with stops in Khartoum and Cairo, and an over-night in Athens which the airline would pay for since they changed the schedule. Hey, great. I get to spend a night in Athens including dinner and breakfast, compliments of PanAm. Back in those days I always tried to get a window seat on a plane. I did not want to miss anything. I remember Khartoum from the air. Brown sand as far as the eye could see and in the middle of the brown sand was a brown city. I am sure it does not look like that today. When the plane stopped in Khartoum the people getting on looked like a cross section of representatives from half the countries of the world. There were two German men in business suits. There was a woman wearing the most colorful African dress who kept adjusting and readjusting a long, long piece of cloth that wrapped around her head. There was a man in a long robe and headdress carrying what looked like a giant shepherd's staff (pre-TSA). There were people wearing all kinds of native dress with all kinds of headdresses. Back then people still dressed to fly. Not like today where it is not uncommon to see passengers in tee-shirts, shorts and flip flops.

But the parade of costumes on that short flight from Khartoum to Cairo was such a treat for me. I never forgot it. I can also remember circling Cairo airport and being able to see pyramids from my plane window. I am sure they look spectacular when seen up close, but seeing them from the air was pretty impressive, too. Back then, Cairo airport did not have jetways. If you wanted to leave the plane, you walked down a moving staircase and walked over to the terminal. I can remember thinking I might want to leave the plane and walk around the terminal during the layover, but the two men standing at the foot of the staircase holding giant guns was enough the make me change my mind. I'd flown around the states a few times by then, and there was that one trip to London and Paris, but I had never seen anything so imposing . . . and frightening. These days, guards, military and security personnel are commonplace in airports all over the world. Back then, it was scary.

But if I thought the gun-toting guards at the Cairo airport were scary, it was nothing compared to the hotel in Athens so generously paid for by PanAm. To quote Bette Davis, "What a dump." The room was not as nice as that seven-dollar-a-day room

I had back in Chicago when I ran away from home. I do not remember what I ate for my "free" dinner, I just remember it was awful. I do remember that I slept in my clothes on top of the bed. If it were today, I would have used a credit card to charge a better room in a better hotel. But back then I had a Master Card, and I do not think it was authorized to be used outside the United States. And I know I did not have enough money on me to pay cash. I came back from that trip broke. But as I look around my home today, I can still see things hanging on my walls that I bought in Africa that I still love.

As of this writing I have been to all seven continents, all fifty states, and over sixty countries. I have always considered myself a tourist, not a "world traveler." I can explain the difference this way: A world traveler goes to the south of France and stays at a friend's villa. A tourist goes to Paris and visits the Eiffel Tower. A world traveler goes to the British seaside and stays at a country cottage. A tourist goes to London to see the changing of the guard. Maybe after I've seen every tourist attraction in the entire world, I'll be able to concentrate on becoming a world traveler.

Meanwhile, back in 1971, cigarette advertising was banned from television; NASDAQ debuted; Amtrak was formed; the Ed Sullivan Show went off the air; 18-year-olds were allowed to vote; Harmon Killebrew and Frank Robinson joined the 500 Club; there was a riot at Attica Prison; Disney World opened; London Bridge moved to Arizona; D. B. Cooper jumped out of a plane; Janis Joplin told us about her relationship with Bobby McGee; and there were nation-wide protests against the war in Vietnam and now Laos.

CHAPTER NINE

In 1972, walking home from one of my night classes, I met Phil, the man who became my husband. Anyone who has ever lived in New York City has seen these street cubicles attached to the outside of a building. Most of them are newspaper stands or fruit stands. The one across the street from my apartment building was a flower stand. As I walked by one night the guy working this stand simply said, "How was your day?" To which I replied, "Uneventful." For a few weeks we would chat as I passed by on my way home from school. We had our first official date on April 24th and were married on July 10th. What can I say? I was 29 and getting bombarded from all sides. "When are you getting married? How come you're not married? Don't you want to get married? You're not getting any younger. You should think about getting married." And on and on and on. I was getting this noise from friends and relatives and co-workers.

In 1972 the women's movement was really taking hold and was going to make us all equal. And that may have been true in the workplace. But in reality, if you were a woman, pushing thirty, and still single, then there had to be something wrong with you. But people would ask, "When are you getting married? as if they were asking, "When are you going to get a new sofa?" As if *getting married* was just something you went out and *did*. I can remember my cousin, who was married at eighteen, started pressing me about getting married when I was only nineteen. So, by the time I was twenty-nine, to her, I was beyond being an old maid. When questioned about my failure to find a husband I would always say, "Well, first I have to get a boyfriend."

Actually, by the time I was twenty-nine I had been seeing someone I absolutely adored for over five years. He was twenty-five years older than I was, but we never had a problem finding something to talk about. He was brilliant and witty and a confirmed bachelor. Plus, although we never talked about being exclusive, I am sure that while we were dating, he was also dating every woman that ever walked across Washington Square Park. So, when Phil asked me to marry him, I jumped at the chance. It was not so much as he *asked* me to marry him. It was more like a statement. It went something like, "I think we should get married." Hell, I did not care how he put it. I could finally get my friends and relatives off my back.

Phil was from Kansas. He landed in New York after getting out of the Navy and had lived there working odd jobs for several years before we met. By 1973 I was pregnant, soon to give up my well-paying Ford Foundation job with all the benefits, and Phil was still working odd jobs. Not the most ideal situation. My daughter, Deborah, was born in November of '73. So here we were. Parents. I was not working. By then Phil was working at an aluminum recycling center in Brooklyn. But somehow, we got by. We never spent money on anything that was not an absolute necessity. Not clothes or furniture. We never ate out or went to a movie. I do not think either of us felt like we were missing out on anything. However, when he quit his job in the spring of 1974, we both knew a serious change had to be made.

We had planned to fly to Kansas to visit Phil's parents in the fall of 1974. However, when he quit his job in May, I suggested that we make the trip then. Kansas. Southwest Kansas. Kansas, for Christ's sake. Fifty miles from Dodge City. I had lived in New York City for twelve years. The stores. The theater. The art scene. The international restaurants. But when we got to Kansas, Phil was offered a job with a local central pivot irrigation company and my mother-in-law bowled with a woman who just had one of her rental tenants give his notice, so there was now this house for rent. A house. A HOUSE!!!! I could not imagine living in a house after living in apartments all my life. A house. Wow! With a yard and a place to park a car and hook ups for a washer and dryer. Two bedrooms. TWO!!! I could do this. I could do Kansas. It would be a hoot, right? I am a willow. I can bend. Phil would work. I would be a stay-at-home mom. We could do this.

WRONG!!! I could not do it. I missed my city. I missed Bloomingdale's. I missed MoMA. I missed the deli . . . *any* deli. My in-laws had never had, or even *heard* of, a bagel. People bought rye bread from the *grocery* store. The Sunday New York Times made it to the library on Tuesdays. And every Tuesday morning I would stand outside the library door waiting for them to open. I missed people who knew what the word *schlep* meant. I missed gay people. I missed art lovers. I missed elevators and public transportation. I missed buildings. I missed that wonderful view from my apartment. I missed lectures and galleries and plays. I missed being surrounded by highly educated people. I missed seeing men wearing business suits with *real* neckties. Shoestring ties do not count. I missed New York's sounds and smells and its tap water. I missed the bookstores. I missed Azuma. I missed the Chinese restaurants. I missed the Italian restaurants. I missed Orchard Street. I missed it all.

Not only that, but I found myself surrounded by people who spoke in these colloquialisms that I never got used to. A wall did not just have a hole in it . . . it had "a hole big enough to throw a cat through." The corn was not just high . . . it was "knee-high to a tall Indian." And (my favorite) the roads were not just slippery, they were "slick as snot on a doorknob." How do you carry on a conversation with people who talk like that? Plus, I never got used to calling soda *pop*, or potatoes *tatters*. And just for the record, the word is inSURance . . . not INsurance. The accent is on the *second* syllable, not the first. And a person from Italy is I*tal*ian, not EYE-talian.

Poor Phil. I was so miserable. I made his life a living hell. I managed to stick it out for two years. But by the spring of 1976 I could not take Garden City, Kansas one more minute. We filed for divorce. I loaded up my 1969 Camaro convertible with everything I could fit in the trunk and back seat; put my two-year-old daughter in her car seat in the front seat (that was legal back then); and headed east and never looked back. My parents were retired and living near Utica, New York at that time. So, I moved there just for the summer. When fall came I would look for a job closer to New York. Not directly *in* the city. Maybe something in Westchester County. Twenty years later I was still trying to get out of Utica.

CHAPTER TEN

In the late 1990's I was still trying to get out of Utica. By then my daughter was living in Washington State, married to her second husband. I was a civil servant counting the years, months, and days until I turned sixty-two so I could retire. A few of the women I worked with had gone to a fortune teller, as a lark, and would come into work the day following their session and talk about what the reader had told them. Some of the stuff was spot on, some rather general and open to interpretation, and some of the findings were just way out there. But it was something that sounded like it would be fun. Ruth was my office mate, but we were also friends outside of work. So, one day we booked an appointment with this "fortune teller" and decided to make an evening of it. We would each have our separate meetings and then go out to dinner afterwards and talk about our readings.

I must say, I went to the reading with an open mind. I mean, I knew a chain-smoking woman, sitting in her dining room, looking at tea leaves in a cup, could not really predict the future. I just thought it would be fun to see what she had to say and to share it with my friend. Her reading started like many of these things do, with a lot of general statements. There were the obligatory letter references: "I see an "R" or an "M" that is very important in your life." There were the generic references: "I see a bridge. Either there is an accident involving a bridge or a picture of a bridge or you live near a bridge." She did say some things that caught my attention. Like she asked if I celebrated Christmas twice. That was true. My sister would always go to Long Island for a few days around the holidays to spend Christmas with her son and grandchildren. When she got back upstate, we would go out to dinner and exchange presents, usually after the first of the year. So, yes, I did celebrate Christmas twice. The tea reader looked very puzzled when she said she could not figure out what kind of place I lived in. She said it looks like a house *and* an apartment. She said it looks like a two-story house, but it also looks like a one-story apartment. Actually, at the time I owned a two-family house. The front apartment, which I rented out, was two stories high; while the back, where I lived, was only one story high. That was a tough one to see when all you are working with is a bunch of soggy tea leaves.

During my session we talked about my daughter, Deborah, out in Washington. Did the reader see anything in that cup about her? Her current marital status? Her children? Just some general stuff. Then as the reader was looking into the cup and turning it around, she said, "Do you just have the one daughter?" I said, "Basically, yes." To which she said, "Because I see another daughter . . . quite a bit older . . . she's trying to locate you." I do not know if it was because the room was filled with cigarette smoke or because I had forgotten how to breath, but I think it took me a full minute to gasp, "WHAT!!!????" I jumped up and walked around to her side of the table and made her show me in the cup where she saw that. She pointed to a clump of tea leaves that did not look like anything to me. I had already started crying. I blurted out the whole adoption story to this woman, a stranger. Needless to say, the session was over.

The weekend following my tea reading I was downstate visiting my girlfriend Jane. Remember Jane? My friend from Yonkers? Only now she was living about forty miles north of New York City. When I told her about my fortune telling experience she was as shocked as I was. She *insisted* I start some kind of search agenda. I did not have a clue where to begin, but Jane knew someone who knew someone who had found her biological mother and so she vowed to track this person down. Meanwhile, back in Utica, I went to a computer store and, for five dollars an hour, I would use their computers to search the internet looking for anything having to do with adoption searches. There were quite a few sites out there, and they all wanted money. They may all have been legitimate organizations. I have no idea. But I had to pass on all of them because I just felt just a little uneasy giving money to some outfit that may just be a scam.

It took some months, but Jane finally got in touch with the girl who had found her biological mother. This girl had used an organization called International Soundex Reunion Registry out of Carson City, Nevada. And they did not charge any money to help with the search. They would accept donations, but there was absolutely no obligation. What could it hurt? I found their phone number on the internet and called them. They, in turn, sent me a form to fill out. Questions on the form required all kinds of information about the child that was put up for adoption. Date of birth; time of birth; birth weight; hospital; attending physician; birth city; name given at birth; name of placement agency. I knew all that information. I did not have it written down anywhere, I just had it in my head. There are some things you never forget. The form also asked for home phone and work phone numbers. I mailed the form back to Nevada on May 22, 1998.

About a week later I was sitting in my office cleaning up some paperwork. It was after five p.m. And the only other person on the floor was my boss, Ellen. My phone rang and the man on the other end identified himself as Tony Scalarti from the I.S.R.R. At work it was not uncommon for me to deal with companies from all over the country. So, when I asked him to repeat the name of the company he said, "The International Soundex Reunion Registry in Carson City." Still, nothing registered. It had only been a week or so since I sent the form out, but I had almost forgotten about it. So, I asked him what the call was about. He said, "You sent us a form trying to locate a daughter you gave up for adoption." Oh, now I remember. The place in Nevada. Of course. He must be calling to clarify some information I put on the form. Probably could not read my lousy handwriting. I said something like, "Yes, now I remember. What can I do for you?" He came back with, "We found your daughter. She registered with us back in 1989."

I remember feeling the blood drain from my head. I remember feeling freezing cold and incredibly hot at the same time. I do not know how I managed to hold on to the phone. I think I said something inaudible just so the man on the other end would not think we had been disconnected. I can remember a million thoughts rushing through my head all at the same time. This could not be real. This had to be a fantasy. These things only happen on television. Thirty-eight years of unanswered questions could finally be realized. Oh my God. Oh . . . My . . . God!!!!!!

The man from the ISRR told me how the information on the form I sent in coincided with the information my daughter (he said my daughter) had sent in. They called the phone number she had on her form, but the number was no longer working. So, they wrote to her at the address listed on her form. He explained that, granted, she had sent in her request almost ten years earlier, but sometimes people stay at the same address and change their phone number. Or, if they move, they have their mail forwarded. He said he should know in a few days if the letter was received or if It was returned by the post office, and as soon as he knows anything he will call and let me know.

When I hung up the phone, I thought I was going to explode. I felt like if I did not share this information with someone I would literally, spontaneously combust. I was supposed to meet my sister at our favorite Greek restaurant in half an hour, but I could not wait that long. I had to talk about this immediately. The only person available was my boss. We did not exactly have a close relationship. In fact, in the fifteen years that she had been my supervisor there was a lot more turmoil than there was harmony. But that said, I still saw her as the type of woman who could (a) keep a secret and (b) offer some empathy. So, I called her office and whispered; "Ellen, can you come to my office?" The reason I whispered was because that was as loud as I was capable of talking at the time. And it was all I could do to get *that* much out. She whispered back with a slight laugh; "Okay." By the time she walked into my office (thirty seconds later) I was hyperventilating. I immediately blurted out, "It's nothing bad. It's nothing bad." She sat down and I said as fast as I could; "When I was sixteen years old I got pregnant and ran away from home and ended up in Chicago, but ended up coming back home and was sent down to a place in New York City that shelters unwed mothers, and I had a baby and gave her up for adoption and a couple of months ago I went to a fortune teller who told me my daughter was looking for me, so I got the name of this place out in Nevada that helps with reuniting adoptees and their birth parents and I sent them this form, and they just called me and told me my daughter also has a form on file with them and they have an address for her, and they wrote to her to tell her they found me." And then I took a breath.

While Ellen took a minute to process all that I had just told her I checked my watch and realized, even if I left immediately, I would be late for dinner with my sister. So, I called the restaurant and described what my sister looked like and told them to tell her to get a couple of orders to go and to have her meet me at my house. I thought there was no way I could sit in a restaurant and talk about this without crying. I can remember telling my sister about the fortune teller, but not about all my other attempts to follow through with the readers observation. Although my sister was my only sibling, we did not have the usual close relationship that a lot of sisters have. We were not estranged and there was no bad blood between us. We just were not close. We lived different lives. I do not think we had any mutual friends . . . ever. If I had to pin it down, she was glass half-full and I was glass half-empty. When we met at my house that night, I told her about the phone call from Nevada. She listened, but there were no hugs or "Oh, I'm so happy for you." I got much more compassion from my boss.

A few days went by and still no word from the ISRR. I think it was ten days after *the phone call* that I heard back that the letter they had sent out was returned to them, addressee unknown. So now what? The man at the ISRR gave me some basic information from the form my daughter had filled out ten years earlier. I had tried to do some internet searches, but nothing ever came of it.

Later that year I took a promotion and transferred to Albany. New in the city, I sought out every activity I could find to entertain myself. I found out about the local theater scene, professional and amateur. I found out where the local art galleries were and visited all of them. I attended lectures at night at the State Museum or at one of the local colleges. I read every line of the entertainment section of the local Sunday paper to make sure I did not miss anything. In the spring of 1999, I was reading about a series of classes that were given at a local learning institute. One was entitled something like: How to Find Anyone. The class description was of a one-night seminar on how to locate someone, given by a New York City ex-cop-turned-private-detective. It mentioned something about lost relatives or people who owe you money, but nothing specifically about children given up for adoption or parents of adopted children. But it sounded like there might be some information I could use. So, for thirty-five bucks I signed up.

There had to be at least twenty-five people in the lecture room that night. The ex-cop, Joe, gave us some basic information about his background and then went on to give us information about ways to start out searches. From the form my daughter had filled out ten years earlier, I already had ninety percent of the information he talked about. I had her social security number. I had old addresses and telephone numbers for her. I had her married name. The only thing I took from the class that might have been helpful down the line was Joe's suggestion that, if you have an old address, go to that address and talk to neighbors and just maybe someone knows where the person you are looking for might have moved to. It was something to think about.

A couple of weeks after the class I got the courage to call Joe down in Staten Island, tell him my situation, and see what he would charge to help me search. He said I had so much information it really should be easy to locate my daughter. He said he would charge $300 if he finds her and, if he had no luck, it would just be $100. I thought that was reasonable enough, so I gave him all the information I had. The very next night he called me and said, "Well, your daughter is not dead. No social security death benefit was ever filed for her. But she's not collecting social security now, nor is she paying into the system. There could be any number of reasons for that. Let me do a little bit more looking. I'll call you as soon as I find something. Just think, by Mother's Day you could be reunited with your daughter."

I do not know how to describe intuition . . . a sixth sense, a hunch, a gut feeling. I cannot think of the right word or phrase or feeling that came over me the minute I heard him say, "Well, your daughter is not dead." But somehow, I knew it was not true. I just knew it. I felt it. I knew what he was saying was wrong. Not that he was trying to deceive me. But just that I could feel that it was wrong . . . a wrong statement.

I did not have to wait long to find out I was right. The next night Joe called. He apologized over and over and over again. He was so sorry. My daughter, in fact, had passed away. I was ready for the news. There were no tears. I listened as he unfolded the events that led up to him finding out this awful news. Apparently, using a city directory, he tracked the old address listed on the ISRR form and connected it to the new address, the address where my daughter's husband now lived. When he dialed the number, a woman answered and he asked, "Is this Mrs. Ravino?" To which the woman on the other end answered yes. He then said something like, "You registered with an adoption location agency back in 1989 and, as it turns out, your mother just recently registered with the same agency." The woman on the other end said, "I think you should talk to my husband."

CHAPTER ELEVEN

Detective Joe was on the phone with the woman whom he thought to be my long-lost daughter. When she said, "I think you should talk to my husband," he was not prepared for the conversation he was about to have. Bill Ravino got on the phone. Joe went on to explain who he was and the reason for the call. He identified himself as a former New York City cop and gave Bill all the information he had on his former wife. It was then that Bill told him about Jayne's death, some four years earlier. She had leukemia all her life, sometimes active, sometimes in remission. She had gone through chemotherapy a number of times and had a very bad time of it. When the disease flared up again, she could not face chemo one more time. Her husband was the one who found her. She had taken an overdose of pills. She was thirty-four.

Bill Ravino was a New York City Police officer. That might have been one of the reasons he had the conversation with Joe, brief as it was. Joe told him he would be reporting to me and asked if it was okay to call him back. Bill agreed, but I think that was only because he was caught by surprise and did not have much time to think about it. Now Joe was faced with the horrifying task of calling me back and relaying all this information to me, less than twenty-four hours after assuring me that my daughter was still alive. I cannot even imagine the courage it must have taken for him to pick up that phone.

When Joe told me all the information he had learned from Jayne's husband, the one word that jumped out at me was leukemia. I had a cousin who died of the disease. She was the only person I knew personally who had had it. Could there be some genetic trait? Note to self: Look up everything you can get your hands on about the causes of leukemia. As I said, I was not surprised when Joe told me Jayne was not alive, but I was totally shocked about the way she died and what led up to it. It was a lot of subject matter for me to digest all at once. When Joe said he would be talking again with Jayne's husband my only request was for a picture. I just wanted to see what she looked like. Joe said Bill had told him they never had children and that Jayne went to a Catholic high school in Queens, but other than that, I knew nothing about her. But if I could just have a picture . . . that is all I would want and then I would not bother Bill anymore.

When I got off the phone with Joe, I called my friend Jane immediately. I told her everything. Still no tears. I could hear she was crying on the other end of the phone, but I could not feel it. We talked for over an hour. We talked about everything Joe had told me. We talked about my cousin who died of Leukemia. We talked about the missed opportunity of me never getting to meet my daughter. We talked about the fortune teller who started this whole thing. And then I told Jane about this mother/daughter reunion I had seen on television quite a few years ago. I did not remember the details of the case, but I remembered the first face-to-face meeting between the two of them. The daughter stepped off a plane. The mother walked up to greet her. They both dropped their purses on the ground and hugged and hugged and hugged. I told Jane that, after seeing that it became *my* fantasy. That was how I was going to meet *my* daughter. But now it was never going to happen. And then the waterworks started. The tears finally came, and it was impossible to stop them. Now that I look back, it was almost a relief.

Joe called back a few days later. He was trying to have a conversation with Jayne's husband, but every time he called, Bill's new wife answered the phone and said her husband was not home. It got to the point where no one would answer the phone. When Joe talked to me, he said he was not surprised. He said if Bill were his client, he would advise him not to have any contact with the person trying to get information about his late wife. Why??!!! What possible reason could he have for giving advice like that? All I wanted was a picture. Well, as Joe explained it, nobody ever wants "just one thing." If I got a picture, then I would want more information, then perhaps a meeting. There is always something else, some other piece of the puzzle that someone wants. Oh, that would not be me. I just wanted a picture. That is all. (How naïve was I?)

Okay . . . let me see if I can use what I learned in Joe's class. What did I know for sure? I called the ISRR and told Tony, the man that was handling my case, about the situation. He said they would consider the case closed and that he would mail me the form my daughter had sent to them back in 1989. At least I could see her handwriting. So, armed with the information on that form and one statement Jayne's husband told Joe, I got to work. She went to a Catholic high school in Queens. She went to a Catholic high school in Queens. Hmmmm. Maybe I could start there.

I called the telephone company and ordered a Queens phone book. How many Catholic high schools could there be? But when the phone book arrived, I found that under "Schools" there were pages and pages of schools, many of them named for saints and bishops and annunciation and immaculate and most holy. Any one or all of them could have been Catholic schools, and who knew which ones were high schools? I did not know where to begin. So, I called Joe and asked if he had any suggestions. Without skipping a beat, he told me exactly who to contact to get a list of the schools I were looking for. I also asked him to suggest what explanation I might use to visit these schools and ask to look through their yearbooks from twenty years ago. Again, Joe came up with the perfect excuse. Genealogy! Everyone is into these ancestry searches. It was a perfect excuse.

Shortly after contacting the Brooklyn/Queens agency of Catholic high-schools I received a pamphlet in the mail showing, by borough, the boy's schools, girl's schools and the co-ed schools. Once I eliminated the Brooklyn schools and the boy's schools, I was left with six girls or co-ed schools in Queens. Just one problem, one of the schools had closed a few years earlier, but it was still open back in the late 70's.

I did not know Queens. I mean, I had been to Shea Stadium and the airports and the World's Fair, but I did not know the streets of Queens or the major highways. Manhattan is so easy. It is a grid, with most of the streets and avenues numbered. Queens is a mishmash of streets with names, not numbers. How on earth I got the courage to drive down there I will never know. When I lived in Manhattan when I was in my twenties, I always had a car. But (a) it was Manhattan . . . a grid, and (b) I was in my twenties. Translation: fearless. Now I was in my fifties and had to tackle this borough alone.

Okay, so here was the plan. I called each of the five schools I was going to visit and made an appointment with each one. Three on one day, two on the next. I think all the schools said they kept their old year books in the library. The plan was that my friend Jane would go with me, but as it turned out she could not get out of work on the first day I was to hit the city. So, I set off on my own one Thursday in May of 1999. Modestly dressed, clipboard, map, change for the bridges. Correction . . . *bills* for the bridges. I was a nervous wreck, but I had to keep asking myself . . . what is the worst thing that could happen?

I found the first school. When I called and made appointments with the librarians, I gave them a time range, like between ten and eleven, explaining that I did not know my way around Queens, and I could not pinpoint my exact time of arrival. So, there I was, outside the first school, and there was not a parking space in site. I circled the block a couple of times and ended up parking next to a fire hydrant. I was about to lie to a nun . . . by comparison, what was a little parking ticket?

I do not know why, but I expected to see a reception desk when I walked in the door. Since there was no one there to greet me, I had to wander through the halls looking for someone in an office. I was directed to the library, introduced myself to my phone contact, and was escorted to a table and chair where all the year books from 1960 to 1990 were already laid out for me. On the one hand I felt like I was committing a crime, but on the other hand I could not believe how easy this was. It felt a little strange to be there with all these girls running around in their little Catholic School uniforms. The one thing that struck me was, like Mary Catherine Gallagher, their skirts were unbelievably short. All of them. I mean, it was a *girl's* school. Who were they showing all this leg for? And the nuns did not have a problem with this? Strange.

I probably spent close to an hour at that first school. I looked through every yearbook from 1970 to 1980. Every page. Not just the senior pictures, but junior and sophomore group pictures, too. Maybe she did not graduate. Maybe she never made it to the senior year. Even though this was only the first school I went to, I felt a little defeated when I left. I was not sure that this was going to work. What if I visited all five schools and it turns out she went to the one school that had closed? Oh, well. Trudge onward. A little bonus: I did not get a parking ticket.

I made it to two more schools that day and still managed to get out of Queens by three p.m., before the beginning of rush-hour traffic. If I felt disappointed after visiting that first school, I was really depressed after going to two more schools and coming up empty handed. What was I doing? This is stupid. I am never going to find anything. But I had come this far. Might as well hit the other two schools, tomorrow.

The next day, Friday, my friend Jane was able to make the trip with me. By now I had the composure of a seasoned secret agent. I got this. I am cool. I can pull this off. Watch and learn. We made it to the first school and were directed to the library. Sister Mary Connors was waiting for us. She sat us down at a table, asked us which years we were looking for, and brought the books out from a back room.

I had noticed in the year books at the schools I went to the day before that they had the name and address of each of the seniors in alphabetical order in the back of the book. So, when Sister put the books on the table, I reached for 1977. Jane took 1978. We both first checked the back of the book to see if the name was there. Jane told me my face turned pure white as I managed to get out the words, "She's in this book."

I had managed to find the ISRR out in Nevada, which led me to taking a class with Joe, which led me to finding the schools in Queens, which led me to this one particular library. But for the life of me I did not know what to do next. I could not think to thumb through the pages of senior pictures to look for the picture of my daughter. It was as if I were frozen. I remember Jane saying, "Do you want me to look at the picture first?" I appreciated the offer, but she could not have pulled that book out of my hands if she had the strength of ten men. You are probably thinking if you were in this situation you would be like a whirlwind, rushing to flip through the senior pictures as fast as you could, eager and anxious to finally see the face you had wanted to see for so long. And that was what I thought I would do right up to the point when I saw her name in the back of that book. Maybe I just needed a minute to catch my breath, although it did not feel like that. Maybe I just needed a minute to calm down, although I knew *that* was not going to happen. Or maybe I just needed a minute to realize where I was and what I was about to do. I do not know. All I know is I was scared to death.

This was it. This was the moment I had thought about for thirty-nine years. I was finally going to see what my daughter looked like. I had not seen her since she was five days old. Over the years I had a mental picture of what I thought she looked like, but I was not prepared for what I saw when I finally got up the courage to turn to the front of the book. What I saw was a seventeen-year-old girl who looked *exactly* like a cross between me at that age and the '59 Chevy. I know you're thinking, "Well . . . duh! What did you expect?" I do not know what I expected. I just was not expecting to see a young me looking back at me from that page.

I wanted to gush. I wanted to cry. I wanted to yell out, "Oh My God!" But I had to maintain my composure. There were young girls all around us in the library working at their own tables. I did not want to alarm them. It was Jane who had the idea to look through the books for the previous three years to see if there were any pictures from Jayne's junior, sophomore or freshman year. They were all there. Group pictures: but, still, we could see longer hair, a different smile. The nun who was working in the library that day was also in the old yearbooks.

So on to phase two of this clandestine plan. Now the trick was to remove the senior picture from the yearbook. I had come prepared with a single-edge razor blade. Sister was sitting at her desk. I had my back to her so she could not see what I was doing in front of me. There were two students off to the right, but Jane was blocking their view. Jane and I started talking to each other without moving our lips, as if we were a couple of ventriloquists. "Is she looking? Can she see me? What about now? Is she at her desk? Are you sure she can't see?" Finally, Jane said, "Okay, she just went in the back room. Go!" So, I carefully drew the razor blade down the full length of the page. It barely scratched the surface. I had no idea yearbook pages were so thick. Again, with the razor blade, and again, the page was still intact. What the hell is this, one of those trick yearbooks, like birthday candles that relight even after you have blown them out? I *finally* leaned into the book and made the cut. I slid the page under a pad of paper on my clipboard. Jane suggested we copy the address from the back of the book just in case some day we might want to drive by the house and see where she grew up. Good thinking.

We thanked Sister for her time and told her, even though we did not find anything, we still had another school to go to. On the way out of the building we passed a small store the size of a closet where students could buy schools supplies. We stopped in and told the girl working there that our nieces had gone to this school and we thought it would be a hoot if we brought them back something with the school name on it. There was nothing. Not a pennant or book cover or notebook. Nothing with the name or logo on it. The only thing the girl had, she said, were some ballpoint pens that were so old the ink had dried up. If I wanted, I could just have them. I took three.

I did not bother to call the fifth school on my list. If I had a cell phone back then I probably would have, just to let them know I had already found what I wanted in another school. As far as I know they are still waiting for me to show up. As Jane and I drove off the island and headed back up to her house I looked at her and asked hesitantly, "Did . . . we . . . just . . . pull . . . off . . . a . . . caper?" She said, "Yeah."

CHAPTER TWELVE

Detective Joe was right. Nobody ever wants just one thing. They always want more. It had been a year since the adventurous trip to Queens. I must have spent a million hours staring at the picture from the yearbook wondering what her life was like. But how to find out? Her husband would not take calls. I felt if I were going to find anything beyond the limited information that I had . . . that the only option left open to me . . . was to write to Jayne's mother and hope, somehow, that she was a compassionate woman and would share even the smallest detail with me.

It took me a month to compose the letter. I wrote it and rewrote it and rewrote it over and over, again. I did not keep a copy, so I do not remember exactly what I said, but I think I introduced myself and told her about how both our daughter and I had registered with the ISRR out in Utah. I know I did not mention going to the school and stealing the yearbook picture. I think I said I got her address form the ISRR form. I must have reread the final letter a dozen times before I put it in the envelope. I even practiced signing my name. It was a big step for me.

On a Saturday, less than a week after I mailed the letter, my phone rang. The man on the other end said, "This is Bill Ravino." I could not talk. I was caught by complete and utter surprise. He said, "I was Jayne Ravino's husband. You wrote to my former mother-in-law." I managed to make some kind of stammering, guttural noise. I got out something like, "I know who you are. I'm . . . I'm just surprised. I wasn't expecting a call."

Once he was confident that I knew who he was he laced into a fit of anger over what I had done. How could I be so insensitive? Did I even think about how upsetting my letter was to Jayne's mother? She was just starting to learn how to deal with what happened and now I have stirred up this whole thing again. He said he never told her about the call he got from Joe because he did not want to upset her, and now I have caused this uneasy atmosphere between him and his former mother-in-law. And on and on and on.

I started crying. Not because of *what* he was saying, but simply because I was being yelled at. And being yelled at by a *stranger*. Well, I think my crying kind of got to him. When he finally stopped yelling, I managed to tell him how sorry I was that I caused Jayne's mother so much pain. Through my sobs I managed to get out how I have lived with this hole in my heart for forty years and when I finally thought I was going to find this child that I gave up so many years ago . . . and then to have all my dreams just ripped away from me again . . . it was just more than I could handle. And, since he was not taking calls from Joe, the only other option I could find was to write to the woman who raised my daughter for all those years and could help me to know whatever she would hopefully share with me about the life of this girl.

He softened. I think he understood that my motives for writing the letter were so emotional and so sincere . . . that there was a longing there that he could not even begin to grasp. Once I won him over (so to speak) he started telling me about Jayne. He told me about her bubbling personality. He told me about her love for drawing and the comic-strip story that he had printed into a book. He told me how she had tried college after high school, but decided it was not for her. He told me how they never had children, but her love for her nieces and nephew was limitless. He told me about her illness and how she dealt with it. He told me his nickname for her. He told me everything he could think of to answer any questions I might have about Jayne's life, and even answers to questions I would not have thought to ask.

He also told me that Jayne's mother had one fear, and that was that she would be at the cemetery and I would *jump* out from behind a tree to try to get her to talk to me. Where did this woman get this idea? But what I could not understand was why she would not want to talk to me. What was she afraid of? I can almost understand adopting parents being . . . I do not know . . . jealous of having their children meet their birth parent. Jealous that the child will have a better relationship with their birth mother than they do with their adoptive mother. But in this case, that situation was impossible. I wanted to thank her from the bottom of my heart for raising this child that I gave up so many years ago. I would think she would want to thank me for making it possible for bringing this child into her life, kind of the way people want to thank the family of an organ donor. I have no idea what I am talking about. I cannot grasp Jayne's mother's feelings. Just as I know for a fact that she could not grasp mine. If she could, she would have been more than happy to meet with me. Maybe it was too close to Jayne's death. Maybe it would always be too close. I do not know.

Anyway, by the end of my phone conversation with Bill Ravino, he had promised to send me pictures and an extra copy of Jayne's comic-strip book along with a copy of some poems she had written. A large envelope from him arrived within a week. Three pictures. One of Jayne; one of Jayne with a little nephew; and one of Jayne and Bill together. She looked quite different than she did in the high school picture. Don't we all?

CHAPTER THIRTEEN

Closure. Who came up with the idea of using that word to describe wrapping up a life experience?

Now that I knew I had all the information I was ever going to have on Jayne, I felt it was time to tell my daughter, Deborah, "my secret." So, the next time I went out to Seattle to see her, I brought with me copies of all the pictures I had. We had a tradition on my semi-annual visits where we would get her husband to stay home with the children while she and I would go to a casino. I first had her come to my hotel room rather than me pick her up at her house. When she got there, I sat her down and said I had something I wanted to tell her. I started crying immediately, but I explained to her that if I were going to get this story out, she was going to have to put up with the stupid blubbering.

I think I started by asking Deborah to hold all questions until I had said everything I wanted to say. And, for the most part, she was able to do that. I do not know what kind of reaction I was expecting from her. I have since spoken to her about what was going through her mind when I dumped all this information on her. She told me that she remembers sitting in that hotel room feeling extremely sad. She felt so sad for me and what I went through. She said it was a lot to process all at once, but because there was so much to deal with, when I gave her the pictures of her half-sister, all she could say was, "What am I supposed to do with these?" We left for the casino.

I remember watching a particular Anderson Cooper show a year or so ago. I watched it twice, actually. Once when it first aired and again when it was a rerun. This show had on two young women who had been abandoned when they were newborn infants. One was left in a bag on the side of a highway and found by a police officer working in the area. The other was found by two boys on their way to school and a woman looking out her window watching the boys kicking a box. Both girls were adopted, and both grew up knowing how their life had started and about being abandoned.

Towards the end of the hour-long show Anderson asked both girls, if they could talk to their birth mother, what would they want to say to her. Without skipping a beat, both of them said they would want to ask her "Why." How could she abandon a little baby the way she did? There are so many other options out there. How could she do what she did? And both times that I watched the show I sat in my living room and cried because I know why their mothers did what they did.

I do not mean to imply for one minute that I *agree* with what their mothers did. But I can almost put my head where they were at the time. We do not know what the circumstances were. We do not know what the household was like where they were living. What would make someone abandon a newborn baby? They were scared. Scared to death. *Overwhelmed* by their situation. Not to mention the fact that they had just been through childbirth, most likely alone. The pain they had just experienced could only have added to clouding their judgment. Not being able to think five minutes ahead. They had to hide the fact that they had just given birth. There was most likely a lot of blood and other fluids that had to be dealt with. The situation, as these birth mothers must have seen it, had to be dealt with immediately. They did not see . . . they *could* not see . . . that taking the baby to a church or hospital was an option. What if someone saw them carrying this bundle? What if someone caught them leaving the baby on a doorstep and they got found out? If you've never been in that kind of situation it is impossible to put your head there. Reason and logic and common sense do not play into it. And I am sure most people reading this are thinking, "Still, that's no excuse." True, being crazy, out-of-your-mind with fear and trauma is no excuse . . . but it *is* an explanation.

But I can tell those two young girls that were on the Anderson Cooper show one thing that I know for sure. Their birth mother has thought about them every day of her life. Guaranteed.

I would imagine there are people out there who fully believe that, when it comes to any kind of traumatic situation, you never really get closure. Or maybe it all depends on your definition of what "closure" really is. It does not mean you forget. It does not mean you forgive. I do not even think it means you have all the answers. To me, closure is a kind of acceptance. An acceptance of the ending of one phase of a journey. And just because that part of the journey is over does not mean that the entire trip is over. Only that it has taken on a different direction. A less turbulent, less confusing phase. A feeling of satisfaction that there will be no more surprises. A "wrapping up", as it were, of all the mystery of the past forty years.

In a lot of situations, the outcome is not always what we wanted, but we can only hope that it is something that we can feel embraces the experience so that we can then move on. And that, to me, is closure.

Made in the USA
Columbia, SC
19 August 2021